Trading Silver—Profitably

Trading Silver— Profitably

DENNIS TURNER
AND STEPHEN H. BLINN

ARLINGTON HOUSE·PUBLISHERS
NEW ROCHELLE, NEW YORK

Manufactured in the United States of America

Library of Congress Cataloging in Publication Data

Turner, Dennis.
    Trading silver--profitably.

    1. Silver.   I. Blinn, Stephen H., joint author.
II. Title.
HG305.T87   332.6'328   75-25888
ISBN 0-87000-290-2

Contents

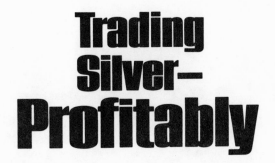

Trading Silver—Profitably

1

Silver in Perspective

WHY IS SILVER SO POPULAR?

For centuries silver has played second fiddle to gold, but the latter 1970s could change that billing: Silver may become as good as (even better than) gold.

Despite the bear markets of the early '70s, silver remains the "darling" of investors and speculators. When the Big Board began its many toboggan rides in '69 and '70, some wags among silver traders remarked that the "precious" metal had become "semi-precious" and had acquired a "tarnished" reputation. But in '72 silver bounced back, its reputation polished a bit, commanding $1.60 per ounce by mid-year. By March 1973 the glamorous commodity was fetching $2.30 and beyond per ounce, and reached $6.50 in 1974.

Why is silver suddenly the "rage"? The reasons vary with the traders themselves, who fall into three general groups—industrial users, long-term investors, and speculators.

Silver has many uses in industry. Photography, electronics, silver plating and brazing, cloud seeding, and battery-making number among the primary uses. And then there's coining, but that has diminished considerably, except, of course, for commemoratives, as nations now use baser metals. Industrial users of silver must carry raw materials in inventory and work in process. Unless they carry short hedges against their inventory, a sudden dip in the price from the initial buy would wipe them out. Silver customers are interested mainly in manufacturing a product for profit. By *hedging* against price changes by *shorting* a quantity of silver in the futures market, they can help minimize the risk of holding the metal in inventory.

Long-term investors and speculators trade in silver for the same reason: to buy cheaply and sell dearly. But *why* silver? Why not platinum, copper, or flasks of mercury? Investors and speculators trade in these and other metals, but nothing to the degree they do in silver. Like gold, silver derives its allure from long association as a medium of exchange and a mark of wealth. Despite the recent worldwide trend toward demonitization—that is, valuing base metal coins and paper money through fiat and legal tender laws—gold and silver traditionally have been regarded as "real" money and "fiat" money only as a medium of exchange. Fiat money is particularly bothersome because it has to be exchanged for something for it to become a store of wealth, and that something is usually gold or silver.

Long-term investors in silver try to protect their wealth by buying the metal in one form or another. They intend to hold it (usually for years), anticipating among other things that inflation and increasing demand will up the substance's price considerably. According to our Charts 1-1, 1-2, and 1-3, the long-run direction of the price of silver may be tending ever upward, especially if the price movements are traced back to the dark depression year of 1932. From a low of 22 cents per ounce that year, silver prices moved erratically upward to the $2 level ($1.50 to $2.50 range) in recent years, and are presently in the $5.00 range.

Although in general silver may be a good hedge against inflation, don't assume that just *any* purchase of it is. Consider Chart 1-1 for a moment. The trendlines of these graphs show that over a 62-year period inflation has grown at a rate slightly slower than the corresponding growth rate of silver prices. During those six decades inflation (based on the Consumer Price Index) has been moving at a compounded rate of about 2.5 percent, while silver has been moving at 3.4 percent per year.

CHART 1-1

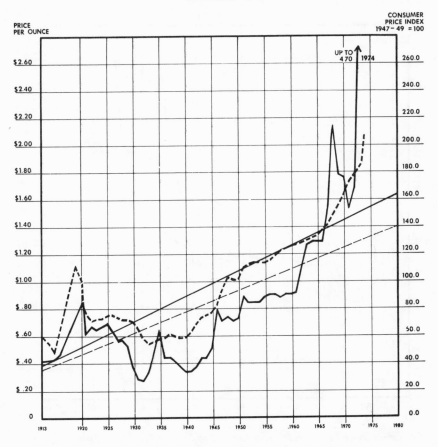

*Consumer Price Index and Trend Line, 1913-1974 (bold and light broken lines).
Annual Average Silver Prices, New York, and Trend Line, 1913-1974 (bold
and light solid lines).*

Although decreasing silver prices will probably match decreasing consumer prices over a long-term period, the former may drop at a greater rate. For the long-term investor, this means holding silver during a recession or depression is risky indeed and probably a bad investment. Why?

First, let's consider prices in general. Supply and demand determine the prices of all goods and services—all commodities,

11

CHART 1-2

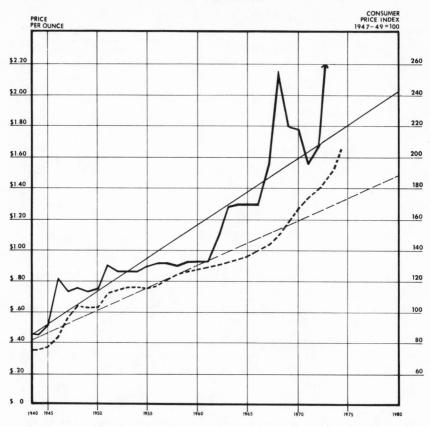

Consumer Price Index and Trend Line, 1940-74 (bold and light broken lines).
Annual Average Silver Prices, New York, and Trend Line, 1940-1974 (bold and light solid lines).

including silver. The price in terms of another commodity—*the exchange ratio*—depends on the supply of that other commodity. More to the point: the prices of nearly all goods and services are expressed by one "other" commodity—*money*. Thus, nearly all goods and services in a particular area are "priced" in terms of the standard monetary unit, and so the prices of nearly all goods and services in that area hinge on supply and demand.

The shrewd investor needs to know more than whether the demand for a particular commodity will increase in the future.

12

Moreover, he must understand and anticipate expansion and contraction of the supply of the monetary unit he expects to deal in because the *money supply affects the level of prices*. Money markets *and* commodity markets should be followed to avoid dire financial losses.

During the Great Depression, for example, the level of prices fell dramatically because of a liquidity crisis precipitated by contraction of the money supply. The price of silver fell along with other goods and services as sellers had to compete for fewer dollars. Since 1941, however, both the money supply (as reflected by the Consumer Price Index) and the price of silver have been rising.

RECESSIONS, DEFLATION, AND DEPRESSION

Will there be another widespread deflation and/or depression? Should either or both occur again, silver's "value" in terms of dollars will drop. In such an event, one would want to anticipate it and dispose of any holdings and invest in high-grade securities in which dollar values would be maintained.

A 1930s-style depression doesn't seem to be in the cards, however. More likely are periodic recessions, or "mini-depressions," during which some industries will post financial losses, some will fold, and most commodity prices will plummet. Recessions (or mini-depressions) occur every time monetary authorities pull back on the money-supply throttle after a full-blast acceleration. Monetary authorities don't have to *contract* the money supply to trigger a recession; they need only halt or dramatically slow down the rate of increase of money in circulation.

An "inflation psychology" embedded in our economic system conditions businessmen and union leaders to expect the money supply and inflation to continue at a rate approximating the one of previous years. If this rate drops dramatically, in effect freezing "new money," then a recession develops. Businesses that depend on constant infusions of new money—in other words, those with inflation premiums built into their operations, including their debt structure—suddenly are caught in a "credit crunch." The longer the economy is without "new money" and *without* inflation, the more serious the economic dislocations.

13

CHART 1-3

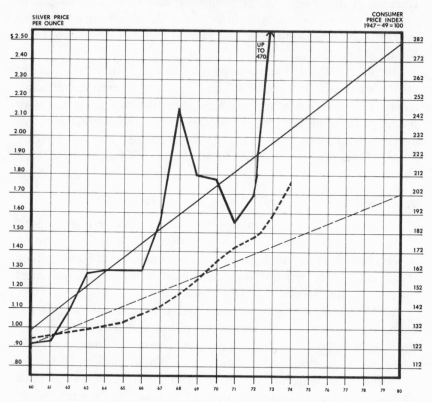

Consumer Price Index and Trend Line, 1960-73 (bold and light broken lines).
Annual Average Silver Prices, New York, and Trend Line, 1960-73 (bold and light solid lines).

BUYING AT "REASONABLE" PRICES

Now, enough about recessions. What does all this have to do with investing and speculating in silver? For one thing, so far as investors are concerned, despite the long-term growth in demand, silver's price is subject to wide fluctuations—soaring during inflationary surges and increasing industrial demand, nosediving when credit dries up and industrial production slumps. For another, so far as speculators are concerned, it means that money will tend to pour into silver during highly liquid periods and tend to leave silver for more stable debt securities during "tight-money" periods.

14

To be successful, the long-term investor in silver must buy at prices that make sense in terms of the long-term price history of the metal. Too often the opposite is true: Amateur speculators and even some long-term investors in silver tend to buy after professionals have staked out positions, during periods of emotional and monetary excess that are justified more by mob psychology than economic considerations.

How can one avoid paying too much for silver? To help, we have prepared three separate tables of "reasonable" prices for silver as a long-term investment (see Tables 1-1, 1-2, and 1-3). "Reasonable" depends on whether the investor is very cautious or very adventuresome. We advise that he not buy silver at a price

"REASONABLE" SILVER PRICES
(BASED ON GRAPHS OF SILVER PRICES)

	Table 1-1	Table 1-2	Table 1-3
1970	$1.35-$1.45	$1.48-$1.58	$1.79-$1.89
1971	$1.40-$1.50	$1.62-$1.72	$1.99-$2.09
1972	$1.44-$1.54	$1.78-$1.88	$2.22-$2.32
1973	$1.50-$1.60	$1.94-$2.04	$2.48-$2.58
1974	$1.55-$1.65	$2.13-$2.23	$2.77-$2.87
1975	$1.60-$1.70	$2.33-$2.43	$3.08-$3.18
1976	$1.66-$1.76	$2.55-$2.65	$3.44-$3.54
1977	$1.73-$1.83	$2.79-$2.89	$3.83-$3.93
1978	$1.78-$1.88	$3.05-$3.15	$4.27-$4.37
1979	$1.84-$1.94	$3.34-$3.44	$4.76-$4.86
1980	$1.90-$2.00	$3.65-$3.75	$5.30-$5.40
1981	$1.97-$2.07	$4.00-$4.10	$5.90-$6.00
1982	$2.04-$2.14	$4.37-$4.47	$6.57-$6.67
1983	$2.11-$2.21	$4.78-$4.88	$7.32-$7.42
1984	$2.19-$2.29	$5.22-$5.32	$8.16-$8.26
1985	$2.26-$2.36	$5.71-$5.81	$9.08-$9.18
1986	$2.34-$2.44	$6.24-$6.34	$10.12-$10.22
1987	$2.42-$2.52	$6.83-$6.93	$11.26-$11.36
1988	$2.51-$2.61	$7.46-$7.56	$12.54-$12.64
1989	$2.59-$2.69	$8.16-$8.26	$13.96-$14.06
1990	$2.68-$2.78	$8.91-$9.01	$15.54-$15.64

above what it "should be" by using the trend line as an indicator of what those prices should be in a given year. Because the prices in the tables are only approximations, a 10-cent range is given as an indicator of what prices "should be" in a given year.

Silver prices, along with other basic commodities, should grow at an annual rate that approaches the rate of inflation. For these reasons, Table 1-1 may be obsolete, unless one allows for a severe depression in his investment plans. That is, if your outlook for the economy is pessimistic, if you want to minimize risk, and your investment is long-term, then don't dismiss Table 1-1. In fact, as recently as March 1972, the spot price of silver ($1.53 per ounce) fell within the $1.44 to $1.54 range given for the year in Table 1-1. It's unlikely, though, that silver prices will ever again fall into any of the ranges listed in this table, for the dollar has depreciated so markedly in the last few years. Only a long, deep depression will sharply lower silver prices.

The most important objection to using these tables is that they are inflexible and cannot take into consideration imponderables such as runaway inflation, worldwide shortages of silver, and monetary panics. Silver prices may well vault into the $6 to $8 range in response to any number of causes. But the graphs and tables were prepared to help the investor gain some historical perspective on silver prices. We have found all too often that one invests in response to overt appeals to his emotions during periods of high silver prices. He is seldom told about silver's past price performance. For example, even in the "good" years of 1958 through 1972, silver's price grew at the relatively modest rate of 5.9 percent annually. If an investor can get a 6- or 7-percent yield in another form of investment, then he is absorbing an "opportunity cost," as well as risk, by investing in silver as opposed to savings and loan associations or bonds. Silver prices tend to move with the economy as a whole, and sharply lower in recessionary periods. High prices lead inevitably to increased exploration, mining, and production as well as better reclaiming methods and searches for substitutes for silver. Silver's upside potential is widely touted, but its downside aspects are usually ignored.

For all of these reasons we think that the potential investor should know that buying silver is not an easy road to riches, nor

16

is it guaranteed protection against monetary mismanagement by the authorities. But because of the traditional acceptance of silver as money, ownership of it ranks second to that of gold as the most basic of investments. Yet even with a clear perspective on silver prices, and even with a working knowledge of the economy in general and the futures market in particular, purchases can be mistimed, resulting in substantial intermediate-term losses.

Fundamental analysis is fine as far as it goes, but it provides few clues for timing purchases or sales, especially for the "gambler at heart." The speculator wants *action*; he wants to make money on the short as well as long side of the market and catch important bull and bear moves during their earliest stages. The *silver futures market* is his arena. To survive in it he wants and needs sophisticated trading methods. And it is for this individual that we show in succeeding chapters how to exploit the silver futures market for *fun* and *profit*.

2

How Silver is Traded

THE LANGUAGE OF THE TRADE

Knowing the language of the trade is imperative before entering a market, especially one on silver futures. So, let's start with some of the most basic terms.

A *commodity futures contract* is a legally binding promise to receive or deliver a specified grade and amount of a good at a specified time in the future. The *contract* is the unit of trading, and for each commodity traded on an organized exchange the *contract unit* is specified. For example, a contract of silver on Commodity Exchange, Inc., in New York specifies 10,000 troy ounces of .999 fine silver bullion as the contract unit. The delivery date is spelled out in the contract, and the month of delivery is an *option*. On the New York exchange, the option months are January, March, May, July, September, and December. A futures contract in silver, then, is a promise to receive or deliver silver in any of the above months. If, for example, the choice for delivery is July, the speculator has a *July option*.

In the jargon of commodities trading, a contract to receive silver is a *long position* or *buy*. If a speculator enters the market to receive silver in December, he has *bought* or become *long* in December silver. A contract to deliver silver is a *short position*, a *sale*, or *short sale*. A speculator in the market to deliver silver has *sold* (or is *short* in) December silver.

19

WHERE THE ACTION IS

A *commodity futures exchange* is a business enterprise. Its functions include bringing together buyers and sellers of commodity futures, organizing facilities for their trading, establishing rules for their trading, setting conditions within which the market operates, insuring honesty and equity in trading, and offering all relevant information on trading as quickly as possible. All trading occurs on the exchange floor by auction. There are no "specialists" as on the floor of the New York Stock Exchange. Futures prices are determined entirely by free-market interaction on the commodity exchange's floor.

At least three commodity exchanges in the United States trade silver—New York's Commodity Exchange, Inc. (or *Comex*), Chicago's Board of Trade, and Los Angeles's West Coast Commodity Exchange. Of these, the volume of trading on the New York exchange is the largest.

Comex decides the options that should be traded and the delivery dates in each option. For example, silver is traded there through the fourth trading day until the end of the option month. A short holder who wishes to deliver may do so anytime in the option month from the first through last trading day. The minimum price fluctuation is 1/10 cent, or 10/100 cents per ounce. As the contract consists of 10,000 ounces, the minimum price fluctuation is $10 per contract. Price bidding then occurs in multiples of 10/100 cents per ounce.

Comex, like the other commodity exchanges, must prevent wild price fluctuations. It does this by placing limits on the maximum price fluctuations that may occur in one day's trading. It reserves the right to suspend trading under extremely unstable conditions. For example, trading was suspended for several days after President Nixon's imposition of wage and price controls in August 1971 because of the uncertainty in the economy generated by these measures.

The maximum daily fluctuation is 20 cents per ounce above or below the previous day's closing price. Ten cents per ounce is equal to $1,000 per contract, the margin requirements. Additionally, the maximum permitted range between the high and low price is 40 cents per ounce, or $4,000 per contract, in any one trading day. Both these rules are suspended during the delivery month. In silver 1/100 cent per ounce is a *point*. So, one point equals $1 per contract, and if the fluctuation is 10 points, then the fluctuation is worth $10.00 per contract.

Commodity exchanges also set commissions charged nonmembers for completing a trade. Entering and liquidating a position is a *complete trade*. There is no requirement to receive a delivery if entering a contract long. At any time before delivery is tendered, the contract may be liquidated by offsetting the position with a short sale. Similarly, a short sale need not lend to delivery if it is offset with a buy. Entering and liquidating this type of position is a *round-turn sale*. For nonmembers a round-turn commission in silver is $45.50 on Comex. The commission, unlike security investing, is not due until the round-turn sale is completed, and then it is charged to the speculator's account. Commissions in commodity futures trading are much lower relative to gains and losses than in stock or bond trading, and with the low margins make commodity speculation attractive.

THE MECHANICS OF TRADING

Floor traders of the exchange—that is, representatives of the member firms—are the key participants in the daily transactions. Member firms often have offices across the nation, better known as *brokerage houses*, and most of these deal in commodities as well as securities and bonds. Since silver is about the most widely and intensively traded commodity, no speculator should have difficulty finding a member of Comex or the other commodity exchanges.

Representatives in local offices transmit their customers' orders to their floor traders, who fill the orders through open auctioning. Trading on the floor of a commodity exchange is quite hectic. Orders are transmitted electronically to the floor broker, then back to the local office when they are filled. Rules of the exchange insure fair trading of orders. All orders for commodity contracts must be entered through a registered representative of the local office or through a specialist's desk.

Associated with each commodity exchange is a *clearing house*, to insure against financial irresponsibility on the part of every member firm. Every trade on the exchange floor is sent to the clearing house, where it is processed against the account of the member firm through which the order was placed. Every order must be placed through a member firm. A nonmember firm must always be associated with a member firm and place its order through it. At the end of each trading day, the clearing house requires each member firm to put up margin money equal to the margin requirements of all the new positions placed through it. This insures the availability of funds to back up the trade of the speculator who placed the order if the price goes down. This margin, in turn, is requested by each member firm of the speculator who placed the order. When opening an account, or while still a new customer, a member firm may require margin funds in advance. After the member firm is assured of a speculator's financial responsibility and character, often it will allow payment in margin to be submitted by check. The firm will advance the margin to the clearing house and "loan" the speculator the money until his check has cleared. However, as the firm is liable for any losses the transaction incurs, it must insist on prompt payment from the speculator who placed the order. If the order is not placed promptly, the member firm will liquidate the position, which it reserves the right to do in the case of margin default by any speculator.

Margin money, then, is necessary to cover losses. If a speculator buys a contract of silver and the price declines, he loses money equal to the decline in price per ounce times the 10,000 ounces in the contract. For example, if the price drops by 5 cents per ounce, the loss is $500. The person on the other side of the contract, who sold the 10,000 ounces of silver, has made $500, which must come from the speculator who bought. To insure that the money is there to cover the losses, the member firm must put up $2,000 per silver contract, which in turn it requires the speculator to put in his account with the firm. If at any time the price movement is so adverse as to cause a loss of half of that $2,000, the member firm will require the speculator to put up additional margin because it must deposit additional margin with the exchange clearing house. The clearing house method of insuring financial responsibility has been quite effective in futures trading. No customer has lost money as a result of a clearing failing to cover a speculator who reneged on a trade.

The margin requirement to secure a position in a silver option is an earnest fee. It is not an actual deposit on the silver. Certainly a speculator going short cannot be required to place a deposit on silver he is to deliver. The margin is an assurance that the speculator has cash to cover losses resulting from adverse price movements and can make this cash liquid at the time the position is terminated. In commodities trading margins generally run from 4 to 10 percent of the value of the contract. Ten thousand ounces of silver at the current price of $4.60 per ounce is worth about $46,000. Yet the margin to secure a contract is currently $4,000 or 8.7 percent. This provides tremendous leverage for profits or losses. A 3-percent change in the price of silver will cause the speculator to make or lose a third of his margin. If the price moves favorably by 15 percent, a profit of nearly 200 percent is accrued, while an adverse movement of 15 percent will cost the speculator nearly twice his margin. Commodity price movements, despite their reputation, are no more volatile than typical stock price movements. The difference is the margin required. In stocks, normally from 50 to 90 percent, a 10-percent price movement, will not drastically affect the size of an investment, while in commodities a corresponding movement would bring large profits or large losses.

HOW TO CALCULATE PROFITS AND LOSSES

Suppose a long position is taken in March silver at 455.70. Two weeks later it goes for 458.90. How much have you made? The quotations you receive in silver prices on future markets are in cents per ounce. For example, 456.50 means $4.56½ cents per ounce. Now the price two weeks later was higher than the entry price, which means a profit was made in the long position.

Two weeks price	458.90	
Entry price	455.70	
Net	3.20	

That is, the contract is 3.2 cents/ounce ahead. As the contract is for 10,000 troy ounces, the profit at this point is 3.2 cents times

10,000 ounces equals $320. Of course, if the price had dropped to 452.50, the loss would have been $320. Suppose a short position is taken instead of a long one. Then the price will have to drop for you to make a profit. If the price drops subsequently, you can buy back the silver to deliver at a cheaper price than you are being paid to deliver it. If you sell at 460.50 and the price drops to 455.50, your profit will be $500. If silver increases to 463.40, you lose $290.

Information on the price of silver can be obtained daily in many major newspapers. No commodity trader should be without the *Wall Street Journal*, because of its daily coverage of futures trading, and the *Journal of Commerce*, which is devoted entirely to commodities trading, foreign exchange, and shipping.

3

What a Trading Method Assumes

CHART "PATTERNS" AND RULES OF THE GAME

There are few speculators or investors in either stocks, silver bullion, silver coins, or other commodities who have not heard the language of the "technical" advisers. Foremost in their repertoire is the analysis of chart patterns. Various types of charts are used for plotting price behavior, including the daily bar chart, the point and figure chart, and weekly price charts. Of these the daily bar chart is the most popular, and hence the most common talk of the trade revolves around price patterns that can be traced to it.

A bar chart is simply plotting daily a line representing the range of prices over which the stock or commodity is traded, with a small horizontal cross as the closing price. Over a period of time these charts form patterns that "technical" analysts believe can be used to forecast subsequent price movements. Patterns such as *double tops, head and shoulders,* and *triangles* are supposed to precede certain types of price movements. For example, a head and shoulders "means" a further drop in price, and a triangle spells an impending price breakout one way or the other.

In addition to the jargon of charting, moving averages and trendlines are integral parts of the "technicians" language. If the price is on one or the other side of a long trendline computed in any number of ways, some bullish or bearish significance is read into this. If a moving average has moved up, or down, a corresponding price movement is alleged to be impending. A price breaking a trendline is a "signal" that the price will be reversing its recent direction. "Profit-taking," "overbought," and "oversold" represent either rapid increases or decreases in prices coupled with reversals. Unfortunately, few speculators are ever able to see the performance of these trading maxims tested. The rules are ambiguous. Any book discussing chart patterns will certainly show the ambiguity on which these methods are based and the lack of verification attending them. The question of how one tells where the shoulders end in a *head and shoulders* pattern is answered with verbal legerdemain, and even admission that the patterns are not so well defined as to eliminate "interpretation." Because the patterns are not well defined, and because they cannot be tested, few can say whether or not they "work." Usually specialists' expositions to novice speculators emphasize the need to employ an experience "interpreter"—one whose services, naturally enough, are only $250 a year. Yet even the "interpreter" cannot tell you if the patterns work. *No one really knows.*

Despite their many shortcomings, though, chart interpretations have some value, and trendlines can help somewhat in indicating future price movements. Behind all "technical" trading methods is a presumption that prices do not move randomly, but are serially correlated—that is, past prices partially determine future prices. The concept is similar to *price inertia*. When prices move in one direction, the tendency is continuous movement in that direction.

If past prices did not help determine future prices, there could be no trading methods that produced profits. For at any given time, a price would be as likely to move in one direction as another. No matter the price's past behavior, no matter how rapidly its rise, no matter the time spent in a narrow range, any subsequent movement would be as likely as any other. A trading method based on recent price history presumes this serial dependence. Chart patterns, moving averages, and trendlines assume that under specified conditions prices will have more of a chance to move one way than another. That most of these chart patterns and

26

trendlines are poorly tested or untested does not alter the assumption behind their use. Explanations for serial correlation in silver price movements are readily grounded in price theory and familiarity with the commodity market process, including the behavior of speculators.

INFORMATION AND JUDGMENTS

A study by the Graduate School of Business at Columbia University showed that only 15 percent of commodity speculators received news more than once weekly on the markets in which they held positions. For most of the 85 percent, their information came from a brokerage weekly commodity report or a subscription advisory service. Fewer than 15 percent regularly read the *Wall Street Journal*, which carries daily commodity reports and price tables. Silver speculators are probably somewhat less informed than the average commodity speculator. One reason is they tend to hold positions for longer periods than average commodity speculators, and their positions are more motivated by political factors than with other commodities. Another reason is that the portion of silver speculators professionally involved in silver processing or silver consumption is lower than with many commodities—say any of the grains—where many speculators are farmers, processors, and storers.

Because of this, judgments on factors influencing silver prices are not made independently by all speculators. Most people strongly depend on, although their positions are not entirely determined by, advice of a subscription service or a brokerage newsletter. Political events also strongly influence the behavior of speculators in the silver market.

Some speculators then follow others in the market. When some act, others follow, either making the analysis of current events more slowly or depending on the analysis of speculators already taking positions. Those who depend on others for analysis will follow, and thus produce serial correlation.

Speculators make varied judgments on the reliability of information, and act accordingly. Some doubt a report's accuracy and do not act. Others require additional verification or wait for possible retractions or modifications before acting. Not only is information received at differing times by speculators, but it is believed in varying degrees. Those who acted early on a rumor may liquidate their position if it is not substantiated, while other speculators had no alteration in their position.

The different objectives of speculators causes information to be discounted only partially, or slowly. Long-range traders and investors will not be influenced by information with only minor fluctuations in prices. Short-run traders and speculators will change their position because of rumors, political speeches, minor fluctuations of the dollar in European markets, a pronouncement by the Secretary of the Treasury, and recommendations by an advisory body that minor price changes will result because of profit taking. Some will act on this more than others, some later than others, some after ensuring that these rumors are true by watching the predicted price change in the market. Serial correlation is thereby caused.

Lastly, technical trading causes serial correlation. It is a matter of self-fulfilling prophecy. If many people feel prices are due to rise when a certain pattern of silver prices exists, buying results and indeed pushes up prices, if only temporarily. These charting techniques have no little influence on short-term market prices. Many large brokerages use technical indicators, charting techniques, trendlines, and moving averages that try to predict on measures of past price movements. When these measures give buy or sell indicators, these brokerages will recommend to buy or sell and then do likewise. Others will follow. Additionally, many large speculators use charting or other technical methods, determining their positions upon a signal indicator. This self-fulfilling prophecy at the very minimum insures serial correlation in the short run upon the silver market, following technical signals used by large numbers of speculators, either individually or through letters of advisory or brokerage houses.

TIME SERIES MEASUREMENTS

A series of measurements taken over a period of time is a *time series*. Statistical theory developed to analyze time series was first applied to electrical measurements and termed *harmonic analysis, stationary processes,* or *prediction theory*. Statistical tools

28

enabled engineers to predict certain aspects of the behavior of an electrical system, without knowing the circuitry, based upon past behavior of the electrical system.

Now, a series of prices is an example of an economic time series, as is a history of production of a good, employment figures over a period of time, or measurements of the money in circulation over a 200-year period. Over the past decade the application of time series analysis to economic time series has made its debut successfully.

Problems involved in projecting the behavior of an economic time series from the past behavioral patterns is far more difficult than with electrical systems. And, it has been only partially satisfactory. Economic time series are not completely describable by past behavior, while with many electrical systems they are. Even if the generator is not known, it will always put out constant voltage through the same circuits, or at least vary the voltage on a precisely cyclical basis. "Noises," or signals that are random in nature and enter through imperfections in the system, are not a major part of electrical systems normally. In an economic time series, most of the behavior is a result of noises of this type—political events, technological changes in production, attitudinal changes in consumers, creation of substitute goods, and poor quality of measurements of the data. Nevertheless, in small local economic phenomena, predictions sought occur far more frequently than major changes in the market or system. Commodities markets are appropriate economic systems for use in time series analysis.

Economic time series, such as a sequence of prices, are generally considered to have four principal components which determine its behavior—trends, seasonal influences, cycles, and irregularities.

Secular Trends. A secular trend is a movement of the price level from one point to another point that occurs over a period of time. It is not influenced by seasonal or cyclical fluctuations but is caused by a fundamental change in the attitudes of suppliers or users of the commodity. A large change in supply relative to demand, in use of the commodity, in availability of substitute goods, will cause the price to seek a new equilibrium. The path to the new equilibrium is a secular trend. It is secular trends that will be most sought by the trading methods offered in this book. A secular trend need not be a large or permanent price movement. In fact, several secular trends undoubtedly occur simultaneously in the prices of a commodity, reflecting changes in short- and long-term supply and demand equilibriums.

Seasonal Influences. Seasonal influences are of no importance in silver futures. Some commodities such as grains tend to have their lowest prices during harvest when supply is largest, and their highest prices when the supply is smallest. However, even in these commodities the markets have become much more efficient due to species that can grow different seasons of the year, improved storage facilities, and speculators' anticipation of the seasonal price change long in advance.

Cycles. It is best to illustrate what is meant by a cycle with a diagram.

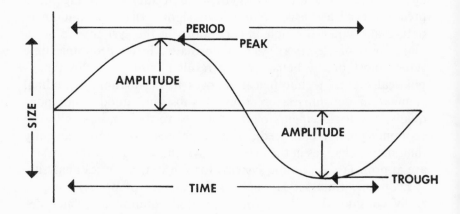

A cyclic movement in prices is one that rises slowly and smoothly until it reaches the highest point. Then it declines past the starting point until it hits a low whose distance from the starting point is the same as that of the highest point. When the price slowly begins upward again until it reaches the starting point, then the cycle has completed one period. The highest or lowest point it reaches is the *amplitude* of the cyclic movement.

In commodities price movements, some of the movement is cyclic in behavior, with cycles of several different periods and amplitudes occurring simultaneously, as with trends. The relationship between the peaks (highest point), troughs (lowest point), and periods is the *phase relationship between the price cycles:* the longer the period of the cycle, the larger its amplitude. In economic time series, the cycles are not well behaved as with electrical time series. The periods vary, the amplitudes change, although their fit to an ideal may be reasonable.

Research in stock prices has indicated that about a fifth of their price movement can be accounted for by cyclic movement. A similar influence in futures prices, when sufficient research has been completed, will probably be found. The influence of cyclic behavior on prices is difficult, but possible to predict through a method of statistical analysis known as *spectral analysis*. Sometimes, though rarely, a *least-squares harmonic regression* can be useful. In other words, the predictors are imperfect as the cycles are very imperfect, and although their existence and average behavior over the long run may be determined, it is not concluded that profitable trading can be based on these predictions.

As this book is primarily concerned with identifying and using secular trends, it is important to note that cyclic movements oscillate around the secular trend as the base line above and below which the peaks and troughs are formed. This distortion leads to improper determination of trend beginnings and endings and, along with the last component of economic time series, leads to imperfect trend identification.

The causes of cycles are disputed. However, one plausible explanation is as follows. New information causes speculators to buy too enthusiastically, and as the enthusiasm wanes, the speculators stop buying and start selling. The price will first move above the trend and then below it, but generally will move around it in cycles. As long as short- and longer-range news causes speculators to change positions in the market, there will be cycles of varying lengths.

Irregularities. Irregularities are price movements that defy statistical methods. Weather changes, price controls, labor disputes, and will-o'-the-wisp speculation are irregularities. When certain advisory firms advocate entering or withdrawing from a market, their advice will cause price changes of a noticeable

31

magnitude. If this advice is based on the analysis of a staff member, and not on a technical method, then this movement can be deemed irregular. Irregularities will distort signals identifying trends. Much of the total price movements of commodities might be irregular. This book therefore concentrates on secular trends, and the signals used to identify them *will be distorted.*

4

Introduction to the Computer Test

SETTLING ON A TRADING METHOD

Once it's decided that silver prices can be correlated serially, and that they can be forecast to some degree by their previous behavior, the next problem is devising the "right" trading method. At first, this may seem an impossibility. But hold on: Just as there are numerous ways of measuring past price behavior, there are equally a number of ways of using measurements to predict price behavior. The most sensible approach toward arriving at a set of guidelines is through the process of elimination.

Forget about any attempts to measure seasonal movements, because silver prices do not have significant seasonal fluctuations. As for cycles, let's shelve them for the time being. Although in statistical theory the study of cycles suggests no insurmountable obstacles, their use is impractical without a computer handy. The size of a cycle is small relative to commissions and errors of execution. When an order is submitted at a predetermined price, that price is not always the one executed. If the market moves while the floor broker is bidding, the actual execution price will be filled at $20 to $50 per contract *away* from the request. Cyclic trading would probably attempt to obtain small price changes from short-term cycles and be frustrated because of execution orders and the $45.50 commission for each trade.

SECULAR TRENDS

Next up for consideration—analysis of secular trends. Moving averages and price channels dot the literature on speculative markets. And, because there are variations of these methods, we have specific procedures for using each method and testing them over fifteen option historical periods. By no means are these methods the best. Conversely, the fact that such straightforward techniques show consistent profits suggests even greater opportunities for the analyst who is familiar with statistical theory and computer programming. We don't claim that *our* variations of moving averages and price channels are the only effective means. Undoubtedly, other uses of them will show definite historical profits. But no law, natural or man-made, can make the market behave exactly as in the past. No one (or one thing) can guarantee the future. And so, the market for silver, as that for any good, has its wild fluctuations and calm periods.

The trading methods selected are robust. The final selection from the variations demonstrated worked well from year to year under a variety of market conditions. We also performed these tests on other futures markets. And, these methods performed similarly in certain other commodity markets, indicating, to us at least, that silver speculators behaved no differently than other types of commodity speculators.

USING THE COMPUTER

The computer program which processed our price data was carefully supervised. It was written in a very powerful version of FORTRAN (formula translator) IV, implemented on CDC (Control Data Corporation) 6000 series machines.

We recommend that any computer research performed be in FORTRAN, the most portable language currently in use.

5

Moving Averages

THE MOST COMMON STATISTICAL TOOL

The *moving average* is the statistical tool used most in forecasting economic time series. A simple linear indicator, it is used to predict next year's gross national product, housing starts, cigarette consumption, even the average height of males during the next decade. Many forecasters prefer moving averages to trend indicators, such as polynomial curve fitting, because they are simple and direct.

Because moving averages have proved effective in industrial and national economic forecasting, analysts now use them in predicting price movements of stock and commodities. Moving averages are used in as many ways as there are analysts.

As Houston A. Cox, Jr., vice president of Reynolds Securities, Inc., notes:*

The basic concept in developing computed analysis is to find a simple formula 1. which eliminates the human factor in labeling market trends, and 2. which can be applied to the most diverse commodities. This formula is required to identify

Concepts on Profits in Commodity Futures Trading (New York: Reynolds Securities, Inc., 1972).

any chosen current price situation as being "up," "down," or "sideways." It has to work equally well in such completely unrelated markets as, say, eggs and copper.

The simplest basic formula to handle this variety of requirements is a moving average of closing prices only. Inclusion of any other ingredient than the close immediate voids the principle of simplicity—labeled philosophically as the greatest of all virtues. This method of determining price trends is not new. It is accepted as valid for measuring trends in any statistic with a known time factor.

The difficulty arises in adapting it to measure price situations where no constant time factor can be found, such as in futures prices which are sometimes fast, and sometimes slow in movement. A short-term moving average, designed to catch every market move, will dissipate its profits in minor trend reversals or "whip-saws." A long-term moving average will avoid the whip-saw, but will miss a great part of a price move. A formula therefore must be selected which contains short, medium, and long-term averages, producing an "average of averages." A satisfactory model, containing the necessary three classic time periods, is a 10-, 20-, and 40-day average, combined into a single weighted index.

This presentation of the moving average as a trading method is typical of those found in books written for the general public. It has several noteworthy features. For one thing, the specific variation advocated (10-, 20-, and 40-day moving average combination) is advanced with no explanation of its "superiority" over other moving averages. For another, no historical testing is presented to verify its suitability as a profit-making tool. Moreover, no price-theoretical arguments are presented to explain why moving averages should work at all.

Most analysts, rarely statisticians, seldom test the methods they advocate, usually because they have neither the time nor the inclination. Apparently moving averages are part of the "conventional wisdom" of the market place. Most analysts cut their eye teeth on bar, point-and-figure, volume, and open-interest charts. Chart interpretation is virtually sacrosanct in the commodity trad-

36

ing community. Yet, its value is debatable partly because analysts forecast differently from the same chart pattern. Chart-pattern forecasting, to say the least, is ambiguous. "Head and shoulders," "double-bottom," and other chart patterns that "foretell" subsequent price movements are not clearly defined. There are no firm rules for defining and interpreting patterns.

Considering the wealth of material available from commodity brokerage firms and advisory services, one is struck by the dearth of studies of the performance of moving averages. This book seeks to remedy that shortcoming so far as silver futures trading is concerned. Each method is comprehensively tested on 15 silver futures options. Trading methods with moving averages that fail are presented along with those that succeed. Each method is defined and easily computed. We attempt to explain why one method works and another doesn't. We determine a strategy for best trading these methods, given the amount of money for speculation.

A moving average of prices is an average of a number of consecutive prices updated as new prices are transacted in the marketplace. Usually in commodity futures, daily closing prices are used to calculate the moving average. The number of consecutive prices used is the *length of the moving average.* So, for example, a moving average of 10 consecutive daily closing prices is a *10-day* moving average.

Let us calculate a moving average (see Table 5-1).

We have daily closing prices of silver futures over a 35-day period and want to calculate its 5-day moving average. Our first calculation will be on the fifth day. First, we sum the first 5 closing prices, then divide by 5 to get the average closing price.

Day 1	138.20
Day 2	138.70
Day 3	140.50
Day 4	139.60
Day 5	141.30
Sum	698.30 ÷ 5 = 139.66

On the sixth day, calculate the average price for days 2 through 6, the last 5 consecutive prices. In other words, the average has *moved*, because it has been updated a day.

TABLE 5-1

Day	Closing Price	5-Day Moving Average
1	138.20	
2	138.70	
3	140.50	
4	139.60	
5	141.30	139.66
6	142.10	140.44
7	140.90	140.88
8	142.20	141.22
9	141.70	141.64
10	142.60	141.90
11	143.20	142.12
12	144.10	142.76
13	143.20	142.96
14	141.80	142.98
15	140.10	142.48
16	142.00	142.24
17	139.70	141.36
18	139.60	140.60
19	138.20	139.84
20	138.50	139.56
21	137.70	138.74
22	135.40	137.88
23	136.70	137.30
24	136.20	136.90
25	135.10	136.22
26	136.20	135.92
27	137.00	136.24
28	136.40	136.18
29	136.40	136.18
30	137.20	136.64
31	139.00	137.20
32	140.10	137.82
33	140.60	138.66
34	139.90	139.36
35	141.20	140.16

Day 2	138.70
Day 3	140.50
Day 4	139.60
Day 5	141.30
Day 6	142.10
Sum	702.20 ÷ 5 = 140.44

Suppose we want to calculate a 3-day instead of a 5-day moving average.

Step 1: Sum the closing prices of the first 3 days.

Day 1	138.20
Day 2	138.70
Day 3	140.50
Sum	417.40

Step 2: Divide by 3.

417.40 ÷ 3 = 139.13

Now calculate the 3-day moving average through day 10, and the following should be your answers:

Day 3	139.13
Day 4	139.60
Day 5	140.47
Day 6	141.00
Day 7	141.43
Day 8	141.73
Day 9	141.60
Day 10	142.17

With this explanation, then, why and how are moving averages used? Notice that the range of the moving average prices is smaller than the range of closing prices. Closing prices range from 135.10 to 144.10—9.0 cents per ounce—in this 35-day period. The 5-day moving average prices, however, ranged from 135.92 to 142.98—7.06 cents per ounce. This is the typical result of extreme prices being averaged in with four others at all times. Thus, the effect of extreme prices on the total picture are reduced through moving averages.

Let's look at Chart 5-1. The dotted curve, which represents the moving average as it develops over the 35-day period, is much

CHART 5-1

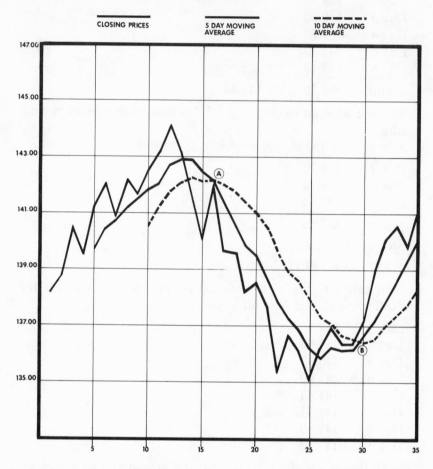

CLOSING PRICES   5 DAY MOVING
AVERAGE

10 DAY MOVING
AVERAGE

smoother than the full curve, which represents the daily closing prices over the same time span. Moving averages not only diminish the effect of extreme prices; they shape the daily price fluctuations into a much smoother curve. A moving average smooths the effect only of cycles and irregularities shorter than the length of the moving average. Although daily irregularities in price fluctuations are smoothed by a 5-day moving average, weekly irregular fluctuations will not be. It is hoped that through this smoothing a secular trend—one that readjusts prices in one direction over a period of time because of a new market equilibrium point caused

40

by a supply or demand change for the commodity at stake—can be defined more easily. Absence of short-term fluctuations makes the price trends clearer and the trading rules more definable. This is why moving averages are used. Daily prices fluctuate so much that they obscure the trend, and that's why they are "noise." A moving average, it is hoped, will average out the "noise" and show a trend in price movement, if one exists. As mentioned in Chapter 4, we assume that past price behavior influences future price behavior. Unless this is assumed, then the existence and worth of trends becomes debatable. Trends precede the use of moving averages, and moving averages, remember, are tools to find those trends. Our computer tests, then, are predicated on the belief that specific trading methods can be employed to use trends profitably.

Don't forget that a moving average has its shortcomings. As Houston Cox warned: "A short-term moving average, designed to catch every market move, will dissipate its profits in minor trend reversals or 'whip-saws.' A long-term moving average will avoid the whip-saw, but will miss a great part of a price move."

Let's refer once again to Chart 5-1. Closing prices peaked on day 12. The 5-day moving average does not begin its decline until day 15, after peaking on day 14—it is two days late. Similarly, closing prices reach their nadir on day 25 and then begin an irregular upward climb. Yet the moving average does not begin climbing until day 29. Here it's three days late—why? Because the moving average is an *average* of the current price *with four past prices. Although the price may begin turning another direction, the moving average is influenced by the past price in its calculation.* Thus, by its very nature it will always be tardy. This tardiness is the cost for eliminating, or at least attempting to eliminate the "noise" of shorter duration than the length of the moving average—the longer the moving average, the more past prices in its determination, the later its response to changes in price direction. Yet, longer moving averages moderate irregularities much better than do shorter ones. Short moving averages are more responsive to changes in price direction, but they moderate only very short-term irregularities.

Moving averages can be employed in trading any number of ways. Since a moving average is supposed to smooth price fluctuations and isolate trends, one method is fairly obvious. When the moving average is increasing, we posit the existence of an upward price trend; when it is decreasing, we assume the opposite. In the first case, we would *buy long*; in the second, we would *sell short*. This is a good method, and experimentation might uncover a minimum amount by which a particular length moving average must increase or decrease in order to determine a trend.

Another popular method is in conjunction with charting. When certain chart patterns suggest a period of congestion followed by a breakout in one direction, the analyst eyeing the direction of the moving average will predict that the breakout will be in that direction. Similarly, in conjunction with point and figure charting, the moving average will be used to confirm a signal. The method we shall be using in our testing employs a relatively long and a relatively short moving average. When the short moving average crosses the long one, we speculate in the direction of the juncture.

TRADING RULES

1. When the shorter and longer moving averages cross *from above to below*, then liquidate long positions and initiate short ones.

2. When the shorter and longer moving averages cross *from below to above*, then liquidate short positions and initiate long ones.

Now, let's move to Chart 5-2. This depicts a 5-day moving average (in broken lines) and a 30-day moving average (in straight lines) as they progress over a 40-day period. Notice how smooth the 30-day average is compared to the 5-day one. Remember how irregular the closing prices were in Chart 5-1?

At A we would have bought a silver contract. At that point, the 5-day moving average, which was below the 30-day one, crosses from beneath to above it. We would have kept our position until B, when the 5-day average recrosses from above to beneath the 30-day one. And we would have held this short position in silver until C, when once again we would have bought long.

If we have a contract in a long position and our moving average method signals a short position, we have two transactions to make. The first is to liquidate our long position, by shorting an equivalent number of contracts (a long and a short contract cancel out). The second is to short an additional position to reverse our direction.

42

CHART 5-2

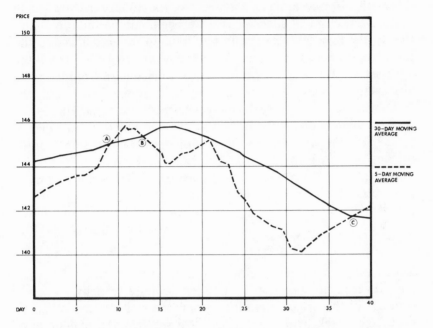

Thus, if after A we were long a contract of silver, at B we would instruct our broker to short *two* contracts—one will cancel the long position; the other will initiate a short position.

Our trading signals are based on closing prices, and we cannot calculate until the market closes. At that time, if our calculations indicate a buy or sell, we place the order with the broker to enter the next morning.

Returning to Chart 5-2, note that A is at day 14. Presumably, we were short a silver contract up to this point. After close on day 14, we calculate the 5- and 30-day moving averages and find the 5-day one has crossed the 30-day one. We then order our broker to buy long *two* contracts at opening of day 15. The execution price will actually be the opening price of the trading day following the day of the signal, not the point at which the moving averages crossed. Remember that we bought two contracts—the first canceled the previous short position, and the second initiated a net long position.

Let us trade this method in tabular form (see Table 5-2). In this way we actually calculate the moving averages and trade the silver market. Notice the table's four price columns—closing and opening prices, and 5- and 10-day moving averages. Our method is the 5- versus the 10-day moving average. As the 10-day average nears in our inspection of silver prices, we begin comparing the 5- and 10-day averages. While examining, the 5-day averages exceed the 10-day. This continues until the 17th day, at which time the 5-day falls below the 10-day. We *sell short*, placing the order to the broker for the 18th day at 139.70. We continue short until the 5-day moving average against exceeds the 10-day one on day 30. A net long position is ordered for day 31—the *long execution* occurs at 137.50. We are now *net long* until the 5-day moving average once again dips below the 10-day one.

We calculate the profits or losses accrued from a trade by simply subtracting the exit from the entrance price.

Enter	Opening of day 18	139.70
Exit	Opening of day 31	137.50
	Difference	2.20¢/ounce

Remember a *short sale* is anticipation of a *fall* in price. Such a fall registers a profit, because the implied promise to deliver a silver contract at the price determined when entering the contract may be bought back at a lower price. We see that the exit price of this trade is 2.20¢/ounce less than the entering one. As we have seen, each cent per ounce per price change means $100 to the contract equity—in other words, a $220 profit.

We see this trade in Chart 5-3. A is where the 5-day moving average crossed the 10-day from above to below, signaling a short sale. B is where the 5-day average recrossed from below to above, signaling liquidation of the short position and initiation of the long one.

Why are two moving averages employed this way? What advantage is there in comparing the employments of moving averages? And, why do we wait until a shorter average crosses a longer one before liquidating the old position and initiating a new one? A longer moving average is used to isolate the character of the longer-term trend in prices. Since the moving average is composed of past prices, it best characterizes the trend of recent prices. Consequently, if the price turns around, the moving average will take time to respond. Notice in Chart 5-3 that when the silver price begins moving upward after day 25 that the 5-day moving

TABLE 5-2

Day	Closing Price	Opening Price	5-Day Moving Average	10-Day Moving Average
1	138.20	138.00		
2	138.70	138.00		
3	140.50	139.50		
4	139.60	140.40		
5	141.30	140.80	139.66	
6	142.10	141.50	140.44	
7	140.90	142.20	140.88	
8	142.20	141.80	141.22	
9	141.70	142.70	141.64	
10	142.60	142.00	141.90	140.78
11	143.20	142.50	142.12	141.28
12	144.10	143.90	142.76	141.82
13	143.20	144.00	142.96	142.09
14	141.80	142.70	142.98	142.31
15	140.10	141.90	142.48	142.19
16	142.00	142.20	142.24	142.18
17	139.70	141.40	141.36	142.06
18	139.60	139.70	140.60	141.80
19	138.20	138.50	139.84	141.45
20	138.50	138.60	139.56	141.04
21	137.70	137.40	138.74	140.49
22	135.40	138.20	137.88	139.62
23	136.70	135.90	137.30	138.97
24	136.20	136.70	136.90	138.41
25	135.10	136.50	136.22	137.91
26	136.20	135.80	135.92	137.33
27	137.00	136.20	136.24	137.06
28	136.40	136.40	136.18	136.74
29	136.40	136.90	136.18	136.56
30	137.20	137.40	136.64	136.43
31	139.00	137.50	137.20	136.56
32	140.10	140.50	137.82	137.03
33	140.60	140.50	138.66	137.42
34	139.90	139.90	139.36	137.79
35	141.20	139.70	140.16	138.40

CHART 5-3

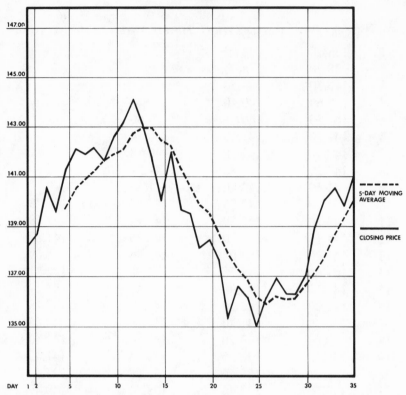

5-DAY MOVING AVERAGE

CLOSING PRICE

average takes a few days to respond while the 10-day average takes 6. Because of this slow response to price changes, a longer moving average may well signal a change in price movement only after the movement is completed or near completion. A shorter moving average has the advantages of being only slightly late and of smoothing out the daily fluctuations because the closing price is used as a one-day moving average. We simply use the crossing of a long by a short moving average as an indicator of a trend change, from, say, downward to upward. The sizes of the short and long moving averages, of course, assume serial correlations in the price movements. The results of our computer tests justify this assumption.* The computer test of Moving Average Methods covered 53 combinations of moving averages, of which eleven have been selected for this chapter. Each combination of moving

*A CDC 6400 with scope operating system version 3.1 computer was used. Programming was written in EXTENDED FORTRAN IV, using the FTN compiler.

averages was tested for its profitability on 15 separate options of New York silver.*

FIVE PROFITABLE TRADING METHODS

The five methods presented below worked remarkably well by traditional profit standards in security investing, ranging on a contract basis from 186 to 308 percent per option life. An option life in silver is 16 to 18 months, so the profit rate per year ranges from 124 to 205 percent. Unfortunately, we cannot expect this high a profit during actual speculation. It is always necessary, it should be added, to keep a portion of the funds in reserve to

TRADING METHOD 5-1

Results of 40- and 5-Day Moving Average Trading Method

Year	Option	Trades	Net Profit	Average Profit/Trade
1968	July	8	2765	345.6
1969	July	13	1905	146.5
1970	July	6	3390	565.0
1971	July	8	300	37.5
1967	Dec.	3	7460	2486.7
1968	Dec.	13	-2375	-182.7
1969	Dec.	9	5825	647.2
1970	Dec.	9	2385	265.0
1971	Dec.	8	460	57.5
1968	Sept.	7	-1135	-162.1
1969	Sept.	11	1455	132.3
1970	Sept.	7	4975	710.7
1971	Sept.	10	1410	141.0
1970	May	4	2460	615.0
1972	Jan.	7	875	125.0

Number of options tested: 15
Total profits: $32,155
Average number of trades per option: 8.20
Average profit per option: $2,143.7
T-statistic: 3.239

*At the end of each option, relevant information on the number of trades, net profit, and average profits per trade were printed.

cover temporary losses.* The methods we found to perform the best are the 40- and 5-day, 30- and 8-day, 30- and 5-day, 25- and 8-day, and the 25- and 5-day (Trading Method 5-1 through Trading Method 5-5).

TRADING METHOD 5-2

Results of 30- and 8-Day Moving Average Trading Method

Year	Option	Trades	Net Profit	Average Profit/Trade
1968	July	6	2055	342.5
1969	July	10	7710	771.0
1970	July	8	3840	480.0
1971	July	8	200	25.0
1967	Dec.	5	8165	1633.0
1968	Dec.	10	−1060	−106.0
1969	Dec.	9	6615	735.0
1970	Dec.	9	4845	538.3
1971	Dec.	9	885	98.3
1968	Sept.	6	−1170	−195.0
1969	Sept.	12	3190	265.8
1970	Sept.	9	5285	587.2
1971	Sept.	10	1850	185.0
1970	May	4	2930	732.5
1972	Jan.	8	890	111.2

Number of options tested: 15
Total profits: $46,230
Average number of trades per option: 8.20
Average profit per option: $3,082.00
T-statistic: 4.010

*After developing all three types of trading methods, we shall present a way of calculating the proper amount of reserve. The methods chosen will minimize the requirement for large reserves by proving themselves not only the most profitable on average but the most consistent.

48

TRADING METHOD 5-3

Results of 30- and 5-Day Moving Average Trading Method

Year	Option	Trades	Net Profit	Average Profit/Trade
1968	July	6	5650	941.7
1969	July	14	–640	–45.7
1970	July	8	4450	556.2
1971	July	8	380	47.5
1967	Dec.	7	7395	1056.4
1968	Dec.	15	–3875	–258.3
1969	Dec.	11	3945	358.6
1970	Dec.	7	4935	705.0
1971	Dec.	8	560	70.0
1968	Sept.	10	–1160	–116.0
1969	Sept.	15	925	61.7
1970	Sept.	9	6065	673.9
1971	Sept.	10	1250	125.0
1970	May	4	2480	620.0
1972	Jan.	8	340	42.5

Number of options tested: 15
Total profits: $32,700
Average number of trades per option: 9.33
Average profit per option: $2,180.00
T-statistic: 2.692

TRADING METHOD 5-4

Results of 25- and 8-Day Moving Average Trading Method

Year	Option	Trades	Net Profit	Average Profit/Trade
1968	July	7	5945	849.3
1969	July	10	6350	635.0
1970	July	8	2930	366.2
1971	July	10	–690	–69.0
1967	Dec.	7	4225	603.6
1968	Dec.	11	–985	–89.5
1969	Dec.	11	4485	407.7
1970	Dec.	9	3385	376.1
1971	Dec.	9	1285	142.8
1968	Sept.	8	1070	133.7
1969	Sept.	12	3070	255.8
1970	Sept.	9	3225	358.3
1971	Sept.	12	150	12.5
1970	May	8	3060	382.5
1972	Jan.	8	1180	147.5

Number of options tested: 15
Total profits: $38,685
Average number of trades per option: 9.27
Average profit per option: $2,579.00
T-statistic: 4.507

TRADING METHOD 5-5

Results of 25- and 5-Day Moving Average Trading Method

Year	Option	Trades	Net Profit	Average Profit/Trade
1968	July	7	6810	972.9
1969	July	20	-2310	-115.5
1970	July	14	2450	175.0
1971	July	10	440	44.0
1967	Dec.	9	3060	340.0
1968	Dec.	13	-1685	-129.6
1969	Dec.	15	4415	294.3
1970	Dec.	9	4155	461.7
1971	Dec.	9	1455	161.7
1968	Sept.	8	-1310	-163.7
1969	Sept.	19	-145	-7.6
1970	Sept.	9	3805	422.8
1971	Sept.	12	1090	90.8
1970	May	10	3800	380.0
1972	Jan.	8	1960	245.0

Number of options tested: 15
Total profits: $27,990
Average number of trades per option: 11.47
Average profit per option: $1,866
T-statistic: 2.812

THREE HIGHLY UNPROFITABLE TRADING METHODS

For the would-be speculator who thinks just any combination of moving averages will do the trick, we present three which, if followed, will wipe him out. The best of these will lose 73 percent in one option. A speculator following it will last two years before going broke. The worst of the lot loses over 200 percent in one option lifetime.

We present these "unprofitable" or bankrupting methods for a reason. Technical advisors in securities and commodities markets often tout a 10-day moving average. A very popular silver letter bases its forecasts on the 10-day average. Two of these unprofit-

TRADING METHOD 5-6

Results of 10- and 1-Day Moving Average Trading Method

Year	Option	Trades	Net Profit	Average Profit/Trade
1968	July	41	3980	97.1
1969	July	62	−7500	−121.0
1970	July	48	360	7.5
1971	July	56	−4590	−82.0
1967	Dec.	23	2145	93.3
1968	Dec.	37	4700	127.0
1969	Dec.	58	−6270	−108.1
1970	Dec.	48	1150	24.0
1971	Dec.	45	−3665	−81.4
1968	Sept.	36	2280	63.3
1969	Sept.	68	−13059	−192.0
1970	Sept.	45	3075	68.3
1971	Sept.	58	−4810	−82.9
1970	May	33	−3105	−94.1
1972	Jan.	44	−2840	−64.5

Number of options tested: 15
Total profits: −$28.149
Average number of trades per option: 46.80
Average profit per option: −$1,876.60
T-statistic: −1.459

52

able methods are based on 10-day averages. We believe a speculator is courting heavy, perhaps swift, financial losses unless he demands proof from the "experts."

Three bankrupting moving average methods are the 10- and 1-day, 10- and 5-day, and 15- and 2-day (Trading Method 5-6 through Trading Method 5-8).

TRADING METHOD 5-7

Results of 10- and 5-Day Moving Average Trading Method

Year	Option	Trades	Net Profit	Average Profit/Trade
1968	July	25	2090	83.6
1969	July	35	−2875	−82.1
1970	July	32	−1750	−54.7
1971	July	40	−6860	−171.5
1967	Dec.	18	−2110	−117.2
1968	Dec.	27	−640	−23.7
1969	Dec.	35	1695	48.4
1970	Dec.	33	−815	−24.7
1971	Dec.	30	−3320	−110.7
1968	Sept.	25	−1400	−56.0
1969	Sept.	39	−4415	−113.2
1970	Sept.	33	−4725	−143.2
1971	Sept.	37	−6285	−169.9
1970	May	19	3145	165.5
1972	Jan.	28	−1930	−68.9

Number of options tested: 15
Total profits: −$30,195
Average number of trades per option: 30.40
Average profit per option: −$2,013.00
T-statistic: −2.682

TRADING METHOD 5-8

Results of 15- and 2-Day Moving Average Trading Method

Year	Option	Trades	Net Profit	Average Profit/Trade
1968	July	17	6575	386.3
1969	July	41	–6045	–147.4
1970	July	28	1290	46.1
1971	July	41	–4535	–110.6
1967	Dec.	9	5100	566.7
1968	Dec.	23	–1755	–76.3
1969	Dec.	30	–370	–12.3
1970	Dec.	32	3240	101.2
1971	Dec.	35	–5565	–159.0
1968	Sept.	18	970	53.9
1969	Sept.	39	–5905	–151.4
1970	Sept.	28	3580	127.9
1971	Sept.	40	–4980	–124.5
1970	May	18	1470	81.7
1972	Jan.	32	–3960	–123.7

Number of options tested: 15
Total profits: –$10,890
Average number of trades per option: 28.73
Average profit per option: –$726.00
T-statistic: –0.657

TWO SO-SO TRADING METHODS

In between profitable and unprofitable are what we consider mediocre, or so-so, moving averages—the 40- and 2-day (Trading Method 5-9), 25- and 1-day (Trading Method 5-10). Both of these gave mixed performances. For example, the 40- and 2-day Moving Average Method seemingly returns a 40-percent profit per year, but it registered a $6,265 loss in its worst year. To allow for this a speculator would have had to keep, say, $6,000 in reserve for every $1,000 contract traded, to insure against going broke if a very bad option occurred first. In this case, the actual return would be only about 6 percent option, or 4 percent per year, not very attractive.

TRADING METHOD 5-9

Results of 40- and 2-Day Moving Average Trading Method

Year	Option	Trades	Net Profit	Average Profit/Trade
1968	July	14	–960	–68.6
1969	July	23	–6265	–272.4
1970	July	14	4110	293.6
1971	July	8	–580	–72.5
1967	Dec.	3	6850	2283.3
1968	Dec.	15	–3945	–263.0
1969	Dec.	14	2180	155.7
1970	Dec.	12	2720	226.7
1971	Dec.	10	–810	–81.0
1968	Sept.	12	–2380	–198.3
1969	Sept.	17	–1555	–91.5
1970	Sept.	11	4545	413.2
1971	Sept.	12	–220	–18.3
1970	May	8	2560	32.0
1972	Jan.	11	–185	–16.8

Number of options tested: 15
Total profits: $6,065
Average number of trades per option: 12.27
Average profit per option: $404.30
T-statistic: 0.455

TRADING METHOD 5-10

Results of 25- and 1-Day Moving Average Trading Method

Year	Option	Trades	Net Profit	Average Profit/Trade
1968	July	17	1235	72.6
1969	July	34	−4070	−119.7
1970	July	36	170	4.7
1971	July	18	1300	72.2
1967	Dec.	13	5380	413.8
1968	Dec.	25	−7205	−288.2
1969	Dec.	35	−415	−11.9
1970	Dec.	23	3615	157.2
1971	Dec.	21	1555	74.0
1968	Sept.	18	−170	−9.4
1969	Sept.	42	−3260	−77.6
1970	Sept.	25	4585	183.4
1971	Sept.	22	2250	102.3
1970	May	22	1590	72.3
1972	Jan.	20	1630	81.5

Number of options tested: 15
Total profits: $8,190
Average number of trades per option: 24.73
Average profit per option: $546.00
T-statistic: 0.638

"THE DRAMATIC EVENT"

Moving averages are not the only means of trading methods which attempt to isolate trends from temporary fluctuations. Such trading methodologies require a *dramatic price event* to signal the anticipated upward or downward trend—an event which historical testing shows to be indicative of real trends, not an index of a temporary fluctuation. In the Moving Average Cross-over Method the "dramatic event" is the shorter moving average crossing over a longer moving one.

In this chapter we shall present an alternative method of

attempting to separate fluctuations from trends, and in Chapter 7 we shall show a refinement of the method that transforms it into a more powerful indicator. At this point it must be stressed that the "dramatic event" discussed here is the *invention* of the speculator or analyst, not an inexorable economic force in the market. "Dramatic events" will often prove to be erroneous indicators, and as the market undergoes fundamental changes, the indicators may have to be discarded. In the short run, at any rate, many losing trades will have to be absorbed over the course of time, inasmuch as a "dramatic event" will often signal a losing trade.

Using the Moving Average Method as an example, suppose that after a vigorous upsurge in the price of silver some profit-taking enters the market, and prices drop in a modest "reaction" to the previous surge. The shorter moving average may cross over the longer one, signaling the initiation of a short position. But if the market is still "bullish," the dip in prices may have been only a "reaction" and the recent highs only intermediate peaks on a long-term uptrend in prices. In that case, the short position may well be a loss as prices advance. Commodity speculators cannot seriously trade without losses, and that's why their objective is to cut their losses and let their profits ride. Our objective is the same in using the methods in this book. According to computer tests, our methods will cut losses and let profits ride, yielding handsome returns on invested capital in the long run.

To explain the extreme price channel method, we introduce a bar chart. Chart 6-1 is a common way of depicting price movements. Each vertical line on the chart represents the range of the price for one trading day. The top of the line indicates the highest price at which the silver option was traded, the bottom represents the lowest price at which it was traded, and the small horizontal line, which may appear anywhere from the top to the bottom of the vertical line, is the *closing price*. A bar chart pictures past price volatility and behavior. More than the closing price, the range of highs and lows permits identification of the area over which the prices are fluctuating.

6

Extreme Price Channels

EXTREME PRICE CHANNELS

A *price channel* is a range within which prices have moved during a certain period of time. The highest price within the specified time becomes the channel's upper boundary and the lowest its lower boundary. For example, a *10-day extreme price channel* is bordered by the highest price and the lowest within a 10-day period. The first 10 days on Chart 6-1 show that the lowest price on day 1 on which the silver option was traded was 152.10, and that the highest at which it traded was 162.20 on day 7. Consequently, a 10-day channel beginning with day 1 would have an upper boundary of 162.20 and a lower one of 152.10.

Channels epitomize the trading method examined in this chapter. A channel is used to determine an area within which normal fluctuations in prices are expected.* Prices that continually move within this area are behaving "normally"—that is, the price movements are assumed to be acting randomly as long as they fluctuate within the channel boundaries. When prices move outside the boundary range, then there's a trend. Channels, like moving averages, change. A given channel depicts the tops and bottoms of

---

*The channel boundaries which "work" have been determined empirically by computer testing.

CHART 6-1

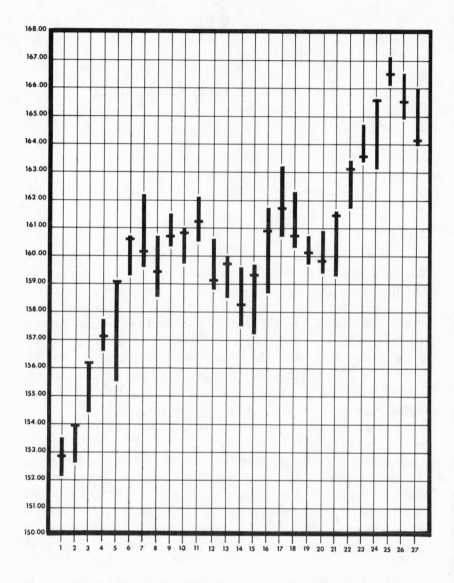

Bar Chart of December 1972 Silver (New York).

60

price fluctuations over a given time. A *channel length* is determined in units of time and may be 5, 10, 12 days. The channel itself will change shape, depending on the highs and lows. This is similar to moving averages where the average itself is calculated over a number of days (40 in a 40-day average), but changes daily as new data enter the calculation.

The second indicator in extreme price channel trading is a period of waiting after the channel boundaries have been determined. This period is a given number of days (depending on the particular method used), moves, according to precise rules, ahead of the channel, and tests the price fluctuations for a movement outside the ranges set by the channel itself. The number of days in the waiting period is also known as its *length*. So, obviously a "3-day wait" is a period of 3 days.

For an illustration of how the Extreme Price Channel Method works, let's return to Chart 6-1. Suppose a 10-day channel with a 3-day wait is used to determine trend initiations. The channel boundary would be the determination. Since we are using a 10-day length, we inspect the first 10 days for that period's high and low. The high channel boundary is 162.20, and the low is 152.10, which occurred on day 1.

The waiting period immediately follows the channel period. In our example, the first waiting day is day 11, the second day 12, and the third day 13. During this period, we "wait" to see if the channel boundary is penetrated. On day 11 the highest price at which silver traded that day was 162.10—nearing but not penetrating. On day 12 the high was 160.60 and the low 158.80—well within our boundaries. On day 13 the price range was again within our 10-day channel.

What now? We now update both the channel and the waiting period. The channel becomes the 10-day period day 2 through day 11. The waiting period becomes days 12, 13, and 14. The process is repeated. In inspecting the new 10-day channel for the high and low boundaries, we find that the high boundary is 162.20, while the low boundary has changed to 152.60, which occurred on day 2 (day 1 is no longer part of the updated channel). We wait through day 14 to see if the new channel is penetrated. On day 14 the high is 159.60 and the low 157.50—no penetration. On day 15 the process is repeated. We determine new boundaries and wait. Another day passes—still no penetration. On day 17 something finally happens. At the outset our 10-day channel would be founded by the high and low of the 10-day period days 5 through 14 inclusive. The high boundary is still 162.20, and the low boundary is now 155.50 (day 5). The price activity on day 17 "breaks out" of our channel—on the "upside." What do we now? We buy a silver contract in the option we are following.

Whenever a channel boundary is penetrated, the trader must move in the direction indicated. In other words, if he is holding a short position as a consequence of following a breakout indicator on the downside, he must liquidate that short position (by buying it back) and initiate a new position long (by buying still another contract) whenever a subsequent breakout on the upside occurs. Orders to the broker are given ahead of time during the waiting period. The broker will be instructed to buy at a price which is a tick above the upper boundary and sell at the price just below the lower boundary.

A few points should be covered to avoid confusion when trading extreme price channels. First, speculation involves either a long *or* short position until reversed. No pyramiding of positions was considered in the testing of these methods, although such trading activity could prove to be profitable. Once a waiting period signals a position, that position remains until the channel is penetrated from the opposite direction. That is, if a long position is held, and during subsequent price activity the upper boundary is again penetrated, no additional long positions are taken.* No additional trading occurs until the lower boundary is penetrated, whereupon the long position is liquidated and a short position initiated.

To explore more fully the process by which the Extreme Price Channel Method is traded, let's follow another example in considerable detail—Chart 6-2, a chart of New York silver futures

---

*The assumption here is that prices are *expected* to continue rising once the initial upside breakout occurs. Continued purchasing of contracts on every new high would *probably* be ruinous.

normally the channel is updated only a day at a time, as we shall see shortly. Looking at days 3 through 7, we determine the high boundary to be 138.50 (day 7) and the low to be 133.80 (day 4). The new waiting period covers days 8, 9, and 10.

What do we instruct our broker? Since we are already long a contract. Both objectives can be accomplished by selling two con- We now want to sell our contract, hopefully at a profit. We wait for the method to tell us at which price to sell. At the same time we sell our long position—liquidating our long—and try to short a contract. Both objectives can be accomplished by selling two contracts at the same price. What price? Let's return to our example. We've determined the lower channel boundary to be 133.80. On day 7, after the close, we instruct our broker to "sell two July silver New York at 133.70 stop, good till canceled." We wait. Day 8 passes and the low boundary is not penetrated. Day 9 and no penetration. Comes 10, the third waiting day, and still no penetration. What now?

We update both the channel and the waiting period, each by *one* day. The new channel covers days 4 through 8, and the new waiting period covers days 9, 10, and 11. Inspecting the channel period, we determine the new boundary low to be the same as the old low—in other words, it has remained unchanged at 133.80 (day 4). Also note that we have already waited two out of the three waiting days—9 and 10. What do we do? Nothing. We have already instructed our broker to sell two July silver New York at 133.70. This is the purpose of the "good till canceled" on our order. If we have nothing to change, our order remains good, saving our broker and ourselves unnecessary time, paper work, and cost. Now what? We wait out day 11—the third day of the new waiting period.

It is now after the market close on day 11. We repeat the process of updating the channel and waiting periods. The new channel period covers days 5 through 9. The new waiting period becomes 10, 11, and 12. Inspecting the channel, we find that we have a new low boundary—134.80 (day 6). So, we instruct our broker to "sell two July silver New York at 134.70, stop, good till canceled; cancel former order, sell two at 133.70, stop."

Day 12 passes, and the low boundary is not penetrated. We update the channel and wait again. We find that the low boundary is the same at 134.80. No new instructions to the broker. Day 13 comes—still no penetration. Our new channel (days 7, 8, 9, 10, and 11) has a new low boundary of 136.20 (day 7). Our new order to the broker is "sell two July silver New York at 136.10 stop, good till canceled; cancel former order, sell two at 134.70, stop."

This process is repeated day by day. It is now the close of the market on day 16. Our new channel (days 10, 11, 12, 13, and 14) has a boundary low of 137.60 (day 12). We instruct our broker to "sell two July silver New York at 137.50 stop, good till canceled; cancel former order, sell two at 136.10 stop."

It is now day 17 (November 22, 1971) and the market has just opened at 137.20 (B on the chart). Since our order was to sell two at 137.50, stop, this means that our order will be executed at any price below 137.50. If lucky we executed our sale at 137.20. We have now liquidated our long position and initiated a short one at 137.20. Having initially purchased our long at 137.50, this means we lost $30 before commission (30 points times $1 per point). Including the commission of $45.50, the total loss would be $75.50— something of a disappointment after all that work and having been ahead most of the time. But, we're seasoned traders and believers in the "system." So, we proceed with our short position.

As before, when we had our first execution, we immediately update the channel to include the execution day. So, at the close of the market on day 17, we update the channel to *include* 17— 13, 14, 15, 16, and 17 become the channel days, and 18, 19, and 20 the new waiting days. The new high boundary is 140.00, and our new order is to buy two at 140.10. This process is repeated as long as it continues making money in the long run.

The next execution comes on day 21 (C). We buy two at 139.80— the price at which July silver opened that day. Our order to the broker would have been to buy two at 139.70. Again we lose money—$305.50 including commission. But we hang in there.

The next execution comes on day 40 (D on the chart). We sell two at 144.10. This time we make $384.50, after commission. That's much better. On day 45 (E) we lose $215.50. On day 60, we make $414.50. Our first five completed trades look like this:

Date	Trade	At	Completed Trade Profit (Loss)
Nov. 8	Buy	137.50	
Nov. 22	Sell	137.20	(75.50)
Nov. 29	Buy	139.80	(305.50)
Dec. 27	Sell	144.10	384.50
Jan. 4	Buy	145.80	(215.50)
Jan. 25	Sell	150.40	414.50
			202.50 Total

Thus, in less than three months we realized approximately a 20-percent return on our $1,000 invested in silver—not bad. The historical results of the 5 × 3 Extreme Price Channel Method of trading are displayed at the end of this chapter.

For those who want to familiarize themselves further with the behavior of the Extreme Price Channel Method of trading, Chapter 11, "Trading Procedure: Following the Methods," has a tabularized format of Chart 6-2, with a description of how to trade using tables instead of charts.

The Extreme Price Channel Method becomes straightforward, once its basic concepts are grasped. Its one weakness, however, involves the problem incurred when price activity during the waiting period turns out to have already penetrated an updated channel. Let's look at Chart 6-3 for a moment. Notice that the price activity from day 1 through day 15 is the same as in Chart 6-2, Days 16 and 17 have been given hypothetical ranges and closes to illustrate the following point:

Assume it is the close of day 15 and that we are long one contract of July silver, having bought it on day 7 at A on Chart 6-3 (137.50). As before, we update both channel and waiting period. The boundary low for our channel (days 9 through 13) is 136.70. We order our broker to sell two at 136.60.

It is now the close of the market on day 16. The low and the closing prices for the day are the same—136.80. Our old channel boundary low, 136.60, was not penetrated. So, we update our

CHART 6-3

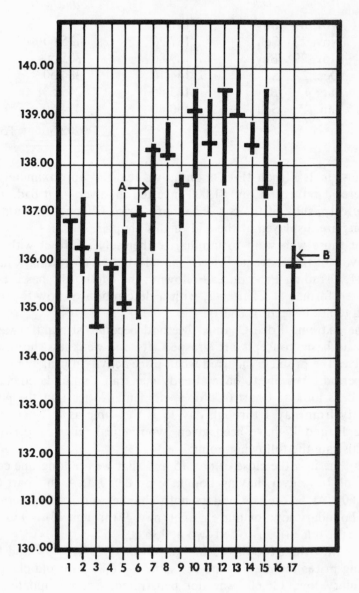

channel and waiting period. Our new channel is the period day 10 through 14. Our new boundary low occurred on day 12 at 137.60. Our first impulse is to continue as before and instruct our broker to sell two at 137.50.

But wait. The market closed on day 16 at 136.80. What happened? While we were waiting for the price activity to penetrate the low boundary of the old channel, it was already penetrating the low of the new channel before we had a chance to do anything about it. What do we do? We cannot instruct the broker to sell two at "137.50 stop." A sell stop order can only be placed at a price below the market; conversely, a busy stop order can only be placed at a price above the market. Since the market price at the close of day 16 is 136.80, a "sell two at 137.50 stop" will not be accepted. What can we do? Following the method, we order our broker to "sell two at the market" for the next trading day. In this case the specific order is to "sell two July silver New York market, cancel former order, sell two at 136.60," assuming a hypothetical market for day 17, this execution is shown at 136.10 at B in Chart 6-3.

Although this variation of trading the Extreme Price Channel Method will occur infrequently, it will occur often enough so that the trader should anticipate it from time to time and check to see that his order to the broker falls below the last closing price if it is a sell order, and is above the last closing price if it is a buy order. Sometimes the updated channel boundary will be such that the penetration price will be the same as the day's closing price. According to Chart 6-2, this happened on day 59. At the close of that day, the channel (days 53 through 57) low was 150.50 (day 53). Our instruction should be to sell two at 150.40. But the close on day 59 was just that—150.40. In this case we again order our broker to sell at the market. *If* the close had been a tick higher at 150.50, our order would have been to sell at 150.40.

In summary, the key to the Extreme Price Channel Method is isolating an area within which price movements are considered to be only irregular fluctuations and in which sudden movements outside the area indicate a price trend. An assumption of this trading method, as with moving averages, is that past movements influence future price movements, and that this influence can be measured well enough so that the speculator can forecast intelligently.

If a waiting period is too long, the chances of a price fluctuation penetrating a boundary greatly increase without necessarily indicating a trend. A short channel measures a small time period for prices to fluctuate. Short channels presume silver is subject to small, sharp price trends.

The combination of a long waiting period following a short channel indicates an unrealistic attempt to catch a short price trend. A signal may well not indicate that a short price trend is underway, but only an irregular fluctuation that will be reversed in a few days.

Yet, a long channel period presumes that silver prices move in long-term trends after fluctuating in a relatively narrow range. If the channel is too long, however, the price will be followed too far in the direction of the trend before an execution occurs. Channels in excess of 21 trading days seem to be too long for profitable trading using the Extreme Price Channel Method. The best waiting period to use in combination with the channel seems to be one of short duration, probably because long waiting periods retain old boundaries for too long. Computer testing, for both long and short channels, in combination with various waiting periods will indicate how silver prices actually trend.

Fifteen combinations of channels and waiting periods were computer tested over the same fifteen silver options tested with the Moving Average Cross-over Method. Eight have been selected for presentation in this chapter.

TWO PROFITABLE TRADING METHODS

Two Extreme Price Channel Trading Methods that returned 18-month profits at 174 and 154 percent respectively were the 17-day channel, 3-day waiting period (Trading Method 6-1) and the 13-day channel, 3-day waiting period (Trading Method 6-2).

70

TRADING METHOD 6-1

Results of 17- and 3-Day Extreme Price Channel Trading Method

Year	Option	Trades	Net Profit	Average Profit/Trade
1968	July	7	1675	239.3
1969	July	11	–3345	–304.1
1970	July	5	6835	1367.0
1971	July	9	3885	431.7
1967	Dec.	8	2830	353.7
1968	Dec.	10	–570	–57.0
1969	Dec.	9	1225	136.1
1970	Dec.	8	4690	586.2
1971	Dec.	9	–325	–36.1
1968	Sept.	8	915	114.4
1969	Sept.	10	–630	–63.0
1970	Sept.	6	6420	1070.0
1971	Sept.	11	315	28.6
1970	May	5	2705	541.0
1972	Jan.	9	–465	–51.7

Number of options tested: 15
Total profits: $26,160
Average number of trades per option: 8.33
Average profit per option: $1,744.0
T-statistic: 2.386

TWO POOR TRADING METHODS

Two methods that register very poor results are the 13-day channel, 7-day waiting period (Trading Method 6-3) and the 9-day channel, 5-day waiting period (Trading Method 6-4). Notice that these methods cited below have 5- and 7-day waiting periods, while the two profitable ones have three-day waiting periods. The length of the waiting period seems to be *more crucial* than the *length of the channel.*

TRADING METHOD 6-2

Results of 13- and 3-Day Extreme Price Channel Trading Method

Year	Option	Trades	Net Profit	Average Profit/Trade
1968	July	7	5945	849.3
1969	July	13	–825	–63.5
1970	July	13	1215	93.5
1971	July	12	4450	370.8
1967	Dec.	8	3065	383.1
1968	Dec.	12	2370	197.5
1969	Dec.	16	–3740	–233.7
1970	Dec.	10	3990	399.0
1971	Dec.	12	950	79.2
1968	Sept.	10	2015	201.5
1969	Sept.	16	–3858	–241.1
1970	Sept.	10	4190	419.0
1971	Sept.	13	2785	214.2
1970	May	9	–225	–25.0
1972	Jan.	11	815	74.1

Number of options tested: 15
Total profits: $23,142
Average number of trades per option: 11.47
Average profit per option: $1,542.8
T-statistic: 2.109

TRADING METHOD 6-3

Results of 13- and 7-Day Extreme Price Channel Trading Method

Year	Option	Trades	Net Profit	Average Profit/Trade
1968	July	7	1675	239.3
1969	July	13	-4635	-356.5
1970	July	13	-885	-68.1
1971	July	12	1950	162.5
1967	Dec.	8	2860	357.5
1968	Dec.	12	-4080	-340.0
1969	Dec.	16	-6000	-375.0
1970	Dec.	10	2540	254.0
1971	Dec.	12	-2590	-215.8
1968	Sept.	10	-2775	-277.5
1969	Sept.	15	-6265	-417.7
1970	Sept.	10	2540	254.0
1971	Sept.	13	35	2.7
1970	May	9	-1705	-189.4
1972	Jan.	11	-1535	-139.5

Number of options tested: 15
Total profits: −$18,870
Average number of trades per option: 11.40
Average profit per option: −$1,258.0
T-statistic: −1.553

TRADING METHOD 6-4

Results of 9- and 5-Day Extreme Price Channel Trading Method

Year	Option	Trades	Net Profit	Average Profit/Trade
1968	July	12	1070	89.2
1969	July	20	−5390	−269.5
1970	July	21	−935	−44.5
1971	July	17	2245	132.1
1967	Dec.	8	4445	555.6
1968	Dec.	18	−2180	−121.1
1969	Dec.	21	−4725	−225.0
1970	Dec.	22	−740	−33.6
1971	Dec.	12	3110	259.2
1968	Sept.	14	−1775	−126.8
1969	Sept.	22	−7380	−335.5
1970	Sept.	25	−3285	−131.4
1971	Sept.	17	1045	61.5
1970	May	13	−1515	−116.5
1972	Jan.	13	1035	79.6

Number of options tested: 15
Total profits: −$14,975
Average number of trades per option: 17.00
Average profit per option: −$998.3
T-statistic: −1.177

TWO MEDIOCRE TRADING METHODS

Without fanfare, and only to show the variety of results a combination of extreme price channels and waiting periods can produce, here are two methods with mediocre results—the 17-day channel, 7-day waiting period (Trading Method 6-5) and the 13-day channel, 5-day waiting period (Trading Method 6-6).

TRADING METHOD 6-5

Results of 17- and 7-Day Extreme Price Channel Trading Method

Year	Option	Trades	Net Profit	Average Profit/Trade
1968	July	7	−1035	−147.9
1969	July	11	−4635	−421.4
1970	July	5	6335	1267.0
1971	July	9	2105	233.9
1967	Dec.	8	1425	178.1
1968	Dec.	10	−3730	−373.0
1969	Dec.	9	−415	−46.1
1970	Dec.	8	1740	217.5
1971	Dec.	9	−1465	−162.8
1968	Sept.	7	−410	−58.6
1969	Sept.	10	−1940	−194.0
1970	Sept.	6	5330	888.3
1971	Sept.	11	−2265	−205.9
1970	May	5	2305	461.0
1972	Jan.	9	−1345	−149.4

Number of options tested: 15
Total profits: $2,000
Average number of trades per option: 8.27
Average profit per option: $133.3
T-statistic: 0.168

TRADING METHOD 6-6

Results of 13- and 5-Day Extreme Price Channel Trading Method

Year	Option	Trades	Net Profit	Average Profit/Trade
1968	July	7	3885	555.0
1969	July	13	-2745	-211.2
1970	July	13	355	27.3
1971	July	12	2890	240.8
1967	Dec.	8	2960	370.0
1968	Dec.	12	-940	-78.3
1969	Dec.	16	-4720	-295.0
1970	Dec.	10	3120	312.0
1971	Dec.	12	-390	-32.5
1968	Sept.	10	-975	-97.5
1969	Sept.	15	-5054	-336.9
1970	Sept.	10	4190	419.0
1971	Sept.	13	815	62.7
1970	May	9	-785	-87.2
1972	Jan.	11	-305	-27.7

Number of options tested: 15
Total profits: $2,301
Average number of trades per option: 11.40
Average profit per option: $153.4
T-statistic: 0.205

7

Closing Price Channels

The Extreme Price Channel Method presented two problems. With the highest and lowest prices as the channel's boundaries, a large risk was taken that a substantial portion of a price trend would be discounted before the method indicated an entry signal. Additionally, once the trend had been completed, a substantial reversal was required for exit. Thus, even if a noticeable trend were signaled, entered, and exited, a loss could well be accrued, as Chart 7-1 illustrates. Assuming a 5-day extreme price channel and a 3-day waiting period, the first trade would occur at A, with an execution price of 148.70 or 148.80. The prices were generally at that or a higher level until B, where a sale would occur with an execution price around 148.40 or 148.50. The trade would have lost about 20 cents per ounce or $20, excluding the $45.50 commission. Yet, in this time a low of 145.70 was reached before a high of 152.00—a $630-per-contract increase. Knowing the bottom and top of a price movement cannot be obtained, it is reasonable to view this short price rise from 148.00 to 150.50, or $250 per contract this way: a real price increase occurred before a price drop, but a loss was incurred on the trade.

To rectify this effect of the rigid trend signals of extreme price channels, it was decided to ease the requirements by constructing the boundaries by the high and low *closing* prices in the channel

CHART 7-1

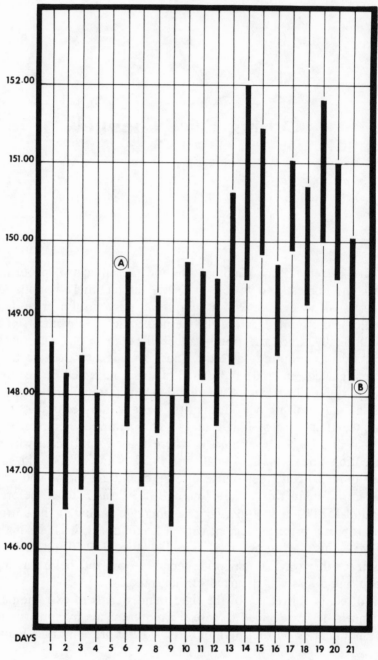

period. For example, to construct a 5-day closing price channel of the following closing prices:

Day	Close
1	158.20
2	156.70
3	157.50
4	159.00
5	157.60

find first the highest and lowest closing prices of the 5-day period. The highest is 159.00 on day 4; the lowest is 156.70 on day 2. In a Closing Price Channel Trading Method the high and low boundaries would be 159.00 and 156.70 respectively.

One aspect of this easing of trend signal requirements is the increased possibility of whipsaws. Assuming autocorrelation in prices as a component of its up and down movements, as well as unpredictable random elements, it would seem that stricter trend signal requirements would decrease false signals. The more liberal the channel, the more opportunity there is for a temporary fluctuation to exceed the boundary channel; otherwise the trading method remains similar. If the price at any time in the subsequent waiting period exceeds the channel boundaries, a trade in that direction is initiated, and those in the other position liquidated. The increase in whipsaws that might be expected from narrower closing price channels might be compensated by the smaller loss incurred with each whipsaw.

Aware that the four profitable Extreme Price Channel Methods had 3-day waiting periods—the shortest tested—and aware of the opportunities of long waiting periods causing fluctuations to signal false trends, the closing price channel's waiting period was reduced to one day. Implementation of this method can be explained by reference to Table 7-1. This table lists the prices of a December 1972 contract of New York silver as it was traded from September 1, 1971, through October 18, 1971. Columns list the date, closing price, the upper and lower boundaries of a 5-day closing price channel, and the high and low prices of each trading day. Also, a column indicates trades that occurred through use of the 5-day Closing Price Channel Method.

High and low trading prices of each day are necessary to know

TABLE 7-1

December 1972 Silver, September 1–October 18, 1971

Date	Close	Upper Boundary	Lower Boundary	High	Low	Trade
Sept. 1	166.00			166.00	164.10	
Sept. 2	166.10			167.30	165.50	
Sept. 3	164.80			165.50	164.70	
Sept. 7	156.50			160.50	156.00	
Sept. 8	155.30	166.10	155.30	156.80	153.10	
Sept. 9	155.00	166.10	155.00	157.90	154.80	Sell
Sept. 10	153.00	164.80	153.00	154.60	153.00	
Sept. 13	152.30	156.50	152.30	153.00	151.00	
Sept. 14	154.60	155.00	152.30	155.40	153.90	
Sept. 15	154.90	155.00	152.30	155.90	154.90	Buy
Sept. 16	156.20	156.20	152.30	156.20	155.00	
Sept. 17	156.30	156.30	152.30	157.20	156.00	
Sept. 20	157.60	157.60	154.60	157.60	156.90	
Sept. 21	155.60	157.60	154.90	156.30	155.50	
Sept. 22	155.60	157.60	155.60	155.60	155.00	
Sept. 23	156.00	157.60	155.60	156.00	155.20	Sell
Sept. 24	155.80	157.60	155.60	156.10	155.70	
Sept. 27	154.00	156.00	154.00	154.50	154.00	
Sept. 28	154.60	156.00	154.00	154.60	153.60	
Sept. 29	153.80	156.00	153.80	154.80	153.80	
Sept. 30	153.50	155.80	153.50	153.50	152.90	
Oct. 1	153.20	154.60	153.20	153.50	153.00	
Oct. 4	148.20	154.60	148.20	152.50	148.20	
Oct. 5	146.30	153.80	146.30	148.50	145.90	
Oct. 6	147.60	153.50	146.30	148.00	147.10	
Oct. 7	148.30	153.20	146.30	148.80	148.10	
Oct. 8	144.50	148.20	144.50	146.50	144.00	
Oct. 12	142.50	148.30	142.50	144.80	142.50	
Oct. 13	143.60	148.30	142.50	143.80	141.90	
Oct. 14	143.80	148.30	142.50	144.50	143.80	
Oct. 15	145.30	145.30	142.50	146.00	144.00	
Oct. 18	146.70			146.90	146.10	Buy

if the price during the time period fluctuated outside channel boundaries, thereby initiating a trading signal.

Channel computation begins on the fifth day. The upper boundary is the highest closing price of the past five days—166.10, that of September 2. The lower boundary is 155.30, the closing price of September 8. Having determined the channel, the trading is determined by price movements on the subsequent day only. Price movements on September 9 determine any market entry. If the price at any time exceeds the upper boundary of the 5-day channel, a long position is initiated. Whenever the price drops below the lower channel, a short sale is initiated. On September 9 the price drops as low as 154.80, lower than the lower boundary of the channel as of the previous day. After closing on September 9, the channel is updated a day. The upper boundary remains 166.10, the closing price of September 2, but the lower boundary is now 155.00, the closing price of September 9. Trading now depends on September 10. As the contract has been sold short, consideration is only given to a price movement exceeding the upper boundary of the channel. On September 10, the highest trading price is 154.60, far below the price of 166.10 required for liquidation of the short sale and initiation of a long position. Now the channel is updated to include September 10 back to September 3. The upper boundary becomes 164.80, the closing price of September 3; the lower boundary becomes 153.00, the closing price on September 10.

Similarly, September 13 does not trade high enough to signal a long position, so the channel is updated through that day. Again no long position is indicated by the trading on September 14. The channel, now updated through then, has an upper boundary of 155.00, the closing price on September 9, and a lower boundary of 152.30, the closing price on September 13. On September 15 the highest price is above 155.00. The contract trades as high as 155.90, so that an execution must have occurred. The short sale is offset, liquidated, by the purchase long of a contract, and a new long position is initiated. The subsequent trading history of the period through October 18 is detailed in Chart 7-1.

Some clarification is necessary here of the order to the broker as the channel is updated. The 5-day closing price channel is calculated after the close of the New York silver market on September 8. It is known that if the September 9 price exceeds the upper boundary or falls below the lower boundary, a trade will be executed. The broker must know this before the market opens on September 9. He is instructed to enter the market long if the price rises above 166.10 and short if the price dips below 155.30. After the short sale, only a reversal is sought. After the channel is updated on September 9, for example, the broker, before opening September 10, receives an order to buy *two* contracts if the price rises above 166.10. One of the contracts is to offset the short sale, and the other is to initiate a net long position.

How will the 5-day closing price channel perform over this 32-day trading period? The first *sell* occurs with an order to enter short when the price drops below 155.30. As silver is traded with a minimum fluctuation of 1/10 cents per ounce, the best possible execution would be 155.20. Assume the execution is not perfect, but 155.10. Similarly for the remaining executions, assume a 2/10 cents execution price away from the channel boundary.

Trade 1:   Sell   155.10
                Buy   155.50

        Loss   0.40 cents/ounce = $40

Trade 2:   Buy   155.50
                Sell   155.40

        Loss   0.10 cents/ounce = $10

Trade 3:   Sell   155.40
                Buy   146.20*

        Profit 9.20 cents/ounce = $920

        Results for three trades: $870
        Commissions for three trades: $136.50
        Net Profit: $733.50

*Here the order to the broker would have been to buy at 145.40. The execution occurred at 146.20 because of a gap opening—a common occurrence.

Comparing the trading record of the 5-day closing price channel with that of the 5-day extreme price channel with a 3-day wait is quite revealing. For example, Table 7-2 represents the high and low prices for the same time period as the closing price channels. It will suffice here to document the trades which would have occurred in this period of time and then compare the performances of the two trading methods.

Trade 1:   Sell   153.00
                     Buy   156.30

      Loss   3.30 cents/ounce = $330

Trade 2:   Buy   156.30
                     Sell   154.20

      Loss   2.10 cents/ounce = $210

For the two completed trades in the September 1–October 18 time period the 5-day Extreme Price Channel Trading Method with a 3-day wait lost $540. Notice that the 5-day closing method for the two trades that occurred about the same time lost only $50. Commissions are not included in either case. Unlike the closing price channel, the extreme price channel did not indicate a buy signal at the end of the period. This is one time the Extreme Price Channel Method proved its worth in avoiding whipsaws, as the price over the next month continued downward. The last long position of the closing price channel would have been whipsawed as the downslide of the prices would have quickly signaled a short position with a few-hundred-dollar loss almost all the way to the bottom of the price movement before signaling a buy.

These two relatively similar trading methods show that a slight variation in rules can yield divergent signals and affect the method's sensitivity to minor fluctuations. Notice that the extreme price channel was whipsawed at the beginning, while the closing price channel, trading on about the same dates, encountered only a comparatively small loss. Later the closing price channel's

TABLE 7-2

December 1972 Silver, September 1–October 18, 1971

Date	High	Low	Upper Boundary	Lower Boundary	Trade
Sept. 1	166.00	164.10			
Sept. 2	167.30	165.50			
Sept. 3	165.50	164.70			
Sept. 7	160.50	156.00			
Sept. 8	156.80	153.10	167.30	153.10	
Sept. 9	157.90	154.80			
Sept. 10	154.60	153.00	165.50	153.00	Sell
Sept. 13	153.00	151.00	160.50	151.00	
Sept. 14	155.40	153.90	157.90	151.00	
Sept. 15	155.90	154.90	157.90	151.00	
Sept. 16	156.20	155.00	156.20	151.00	
Sept. 17	157.20	156.00			
Sept. 20	157.60	156.90			
Sept. 21	156.30	155.50	157.60	154.90	Buy
Sept. 22	155.60	155.00	157.60	154.90	
Sept. 23	156.00	155.20			
Sept. 24	156.10	155.70			
Sept. 27	154.50	154.00	156.30	154.00	Sell
Sept. 28	154.60	153.60	156.10	153.60	
Sept. 29	154.80	153.80	156.10	153.60	
Sept. 30	153.50	152.90	156.10	152.90	
Oct. 1	153.50	153.00	154.80	152.90	
Oct. 4	152.50	148.20	154.80	148.20	
Oct. 5	148.50	145.90	154.80	145.90	
Oct. 6	148.00	147.10	153.50	145.90	
Oct. 7	148.80	148.10	153.50	145.90	
Oct. 8	146.50	144.00	152.50	144.00	
Oct. 12	144.80	142.50	148.80	142.50	
Oct. 13	143.80	141.90	148.80	141.90	
Oct. 14	144.50	143.80			
Oct. 15	146.00	144.00			
Oct. 18	146.90	146.10			

CHART 7-2

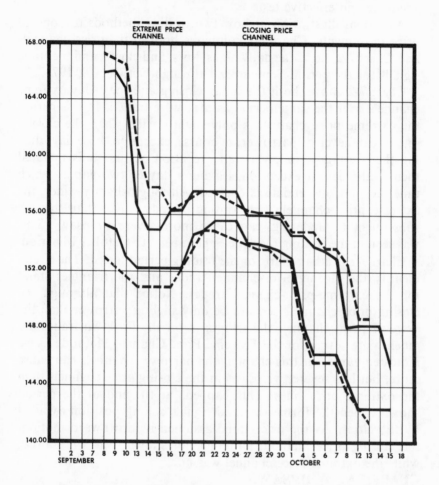

EXTREME PRICE CHANNEL

CLOSING PRICE CHANNEL

sensitivity to minor fluctuations caused it to be whipsawed while the stricter requirements on trend identification allowed the extreme price channel to avoid a reversal on this same minor fluctuation. The major weakness of the extreme price channel seems to be its width. Because of the channel's breadth, too much of a price movement will occur before the trend is signaled. The major weakness of the closing price channel is that its narrowness causes sensitivity to minor fluctuations that lead to whipsaws. This comparison is intended to instill in the reader a healthy dis-

85

trust of "experts" who tout a trading method without providing adequate and effective tests.

As a final illustration of how two trading methods respond to price movements, Chart 7-1 compares both of the price channels and Chart 7-2 shows the daily highs, lows, and closes, and the trade signals for the period September 1 through October 18, 1971.

Chart 7-2 shows both the 5-day closing and the 5-day extreme channels over the same period as they were traded. In this period the extreme price channel is only slightly wider than the closing one. It can never be narrower, of course, except on those days during the waiting period when an execution occurs. It is updated then to the day of execution, leaving a day or two gap at which time the previous update is charted. Although slightly wider, the extreme price channel, with waiting periods longer than the day subsequent to updating, can cause more severe whipsaws. This was seen in the trading over the September 1 to October 18 period.

Chart 7-3 is a bar chart for the trading period tested. The circles identify the closing-price-channel trades and the triangles stand for the extreme-price-channel trades. Notice that although the closing price channel seems to be only slightly narrower than the extreme price channel, the whipsaws on the first two trades are much more severe for the Extreme Price Channel Method. As we indicated earlier in this chapter, the narrower channels can cause more, but less severe, whipsaws in the closing price channels than the extreme price ones. This happens at the end of the period shown, when the former method signals a long position avoided by the latter. As the price trend assumed its downward motion, the closing price method, although not shown, was whipsawed, while the extreme price channel was not.

CLASSICAL WHIPSAWS

Last for illustrative purposes are two examples of classical whipsaws. No speculator can hope to avoid them, but through judicious trading he can reduce the number encountered. This is one reason why sufficient reserves must be kept in an account. Chart 7-4 shows a hypothetical whipsaw of an extreme price channel on the left, and a closing price channel on the right. The pattern is simple. The method has given false signals, assuming a fluctuation was actually a trend, has entered the position long and suffered an immediate reversal in price. The reversal is sufficient to signal a

CHART 7-3

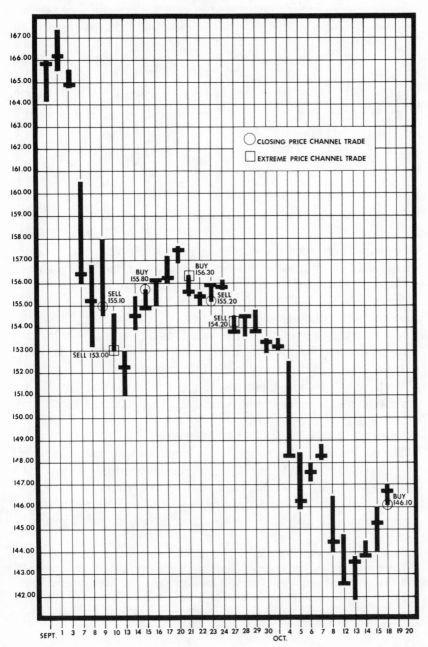

○ CLOSING PRICE CHANNEL TRADE

☐ EXTREME PRICE CHANNEL TRADE

BUY 155.80

BUY 156.30

SELL 155.10

SELL 155.20

SELL 154.20

SELL 153.00

BUY 146.10

CHART 7-4

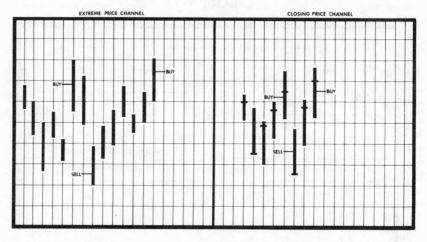

short sale. The price movement reverses itself again sufficiently to signal a long position. Two quick losses are taken. Here we have a classical whipsaw. In the Closing Price Channel Method the losses will be smaller, but whipsaws are more likely to occur. Despite the shortcomings discussed thus far, closing price channels perform much better than the other two methods presented. Whipsaws occur so rarely that they don't seriously affect the profitable trading resulting from early trend identification.

Seven closing price channels tested are presented here. The same information was displayed and tested on the Extreme Price Channel and Moving Average Methods.*

SIX PROFITABLE TRADING METHODS

The profitable methods are: 37-day closing price channel, 33-day, 21-day, 17-day, 13-day, and 9-day (Trading Method 7-1 through Trading Method 7-6). Profits per option ranged from 178 to 350 percent. Notice that the shorter channels generally outperformed the longer channels, the 9-day closing price one returning 350 percent.

---

*The computer and language used in programming the tests were identical to those used in the previous tests. The operating system used by the computer was changed to a computer-center-originated version called Calidoscope, which improved certain features of Scope, particularly multivariable task programming and extra core storage. Change in interaction between the FORTRAN compiler and the operating system was minimal.

However, almost all the channel periods producing profits lends great credence to the description of commodity price movements as a mixture of trends among irregular fluctuations. Apparently a channel can be an effective method of isolating the trend from the fluctuations.

TRADING METHOD 7-1

Results of 37-Day Closing Price Channel Trading Method

Year	Option	Trades	Net Profit	Average Profit/Trade
1968	July	5	−225	−45.0
1969	July	2	6160	3080.0
1970	July	3	4395	1465.0
1971	July	5	1245	249.0
1967	Dec.	4	1340	335.0
1968	Dec.	4	3165	791.2
1969	Dec.	3	4825	1608.3
1970	Dec.	4	880	220.0
1971	Dec.	5	−1125	−225.0
1968	Sept.	4	1500	375.0
1969	Sept.	2	7650	3825.0
1970	Sept.	6	880	146.7
1971	Sept.	5	915	183.0
1970	May	3	−425	−141.7
1972	Jan.	3	1155	385.0

Number of options tested: 15
Total profits: $32,335
Average number of trades per option: 3.87
Average profit per option: $2,155.7
T-statistic: 3.289

TRADING METHOD 7-2

Results of 33-Day Closing Price Channel Trading Method

Year	Option	Trades	Net Profit	Average Profit/Trade
1968	July	5	435	87.0
1969	July	2	6160	3080.0
1970	July	5	3595	719.0
1971	July	9	−2055	−228.3
1967	Dec.	4	2335	583.7
1968	Dec.	4	3915	978.7
1969	Dec.	3	6285	2095.0
1970	Dec.	8	−1220	−152.5
1971	Dec.	5	−345	−69.0
1968	Sept.	4	3190	797.5
1969	Sept.	4	2860	715.0
1970	Sept.	6	1490	248.3
1971	Sept.	7	−1195	−170.7
1970	May	3	645	215.0
1972	Jan.	4	610	152.5

Number of options tested: 15
Total profits: $26,705
Average number of trades per option: 4.87
Average profit per option: $1,780.3
T-statistic: 2.684

TRADING METHOD 7-3

Results of 21-Day Closing Price Channel Trading Method

Year	Option	Trades	Net Profit	Average Profit/Trade
1968	July	7	950	135.7
1969	July	9	−235	−26.1
1970	July	7	4515	645.0
1971	July	9	3945	438.3
1967	Dec.	7	2110	301.4
1968	Dec.	8	725	90.6
1969	Dec.	7	2395	342.1
1970	Dec.	8	3180	397.5
1971	Dec.	9	−185	−20.6
1968	Sept.	6	3755	625.8
1969	Sept.	6	3420	570.0
1970	Sept.	8	4310	538.7
1971	Sept.	11	165	15.0
1970	May	3	4675	1558.3
1972	Jan.	8	−660	−82.5

Number of options tested: 15
Total profits: $33,005
Average number of trades per option: 7.53
Average profit per option: $2,204.3
T-statistic: 4.448

TRADING METHOD 7-4

Results of 17-Day Closing Price Channel Trading Method

Year	Option	Trades	Net Profit	Average Profit/Trade
1968	July	7	4270	610.0
1969	July	13	−1535	−118.1
1970	July	7	6055	865.0
1971	July	9	5785	642.8
1967	Dec.	8	3310	413.7
1968	Dec.	10	1870	187.0
1969	Dec.	13	−1555	−119.6
1970	Dec.	8	5720	715.0
1971	Dec.	9	2275	252.8
1968	Sept.	8	3485	435.6
1969	Sept.	12	−519	−43.2
1970	Sept.	10	4350	435.0
1971	Sept.	11	2015	183.2
1970	May	9	−995	−110.6
1972	Jan.	9	1155	128.3

Number of options tested: 15
Total Profits: $35,686
Average number of trades per option: 9.53
Average profit per option: $2,379.1
T-statistic: 3.477

TRADING METHOD 7-5

Results of 13-Day Closing Price Channel Trading Method

Year	Option	Trades	Net Profit	Average Profit/Trade
1968	July	9	4420	491.1
1969	July	14	3150	225.0
1970	July	18	1740	96.7
1971	July	14	5680	405.7
1967	Dec.	8	5025	628.1
1968	Dec.	14	1180	84.3
1969	Dec.	16	1360	85.0
1970	Dec.	14	4490	320.7
1971	Dec.	14	1830	130.7
1968	Sept.	12	1415	117.9
1969	Sept.	16	1112	69.5
1970	Sept.	14	5120	365.7
1971	Sept.	15	3725	248.3
1970	May	9	1775	197.2
1972	Jan.	15	955	63.7

Number of options tested: 15
Total profits: $42,977
Average number of trades per option: 13.47
Average profit per option: $2,865.1
T-statistic: 6.484

TRADING METHOD 7-6

Results of 9-Day Closing Price Channel Trading Method

Year	Option	Trades	Net Profit	Average Profit/Trade
1968	July	16	4160	260.0
1969	July	21	4525	215.5
1970	July	28	1140	40.7
1971	July	26	1860	71.5
1967	Dec.	8	7925	990.6
1968	Dec.	20	7710	385.5
1969	Dec.	25	1815	72.6
1970	Dec.	22	6380	290.0
1971	Dec.	21	1645	78.3
1968	Sept.	14	6830	487.9
1969	Sept.	23	4125	179.3
1970	Sept.	32	1040	32.5
1971	Sept.	30	−690	−23.0
1970	May	15	2695	179.7
1972	Jan.	19	1395	73.4

Number of options tested: 15
Total profits: $52,555
Average number of trades per option: 21.33
Average profit per option: $3,503.7
T-statistic: 5.032

TRADING METHOD 7-7

Results of 29-Day Closing Price Channel Trading Method

Year	Option	Trades	Net Profit	Average Profit/Trade
1968	July	7	−5770	−824.3
1969	July	4	2020	505.0
1970	July	5	4215	843.0
1971	July	9	15	1.7
1967	Dec.	4	2900	725.0
1968	Dec.	7	−4370	−624.3
1969	Dec.	5	2635	527.0
1970	Dec.	8	−90	−11.2
1971	Dec.	7	−2115	−302.1
1968	Sept.	6	−3075	−512.5
1969	Sept.	4	3320	830.0
1970	Sept.	6	2930	488.3
1971	Sept.	11	−4575	−415.9
1970	May	3	2345	781.7
1972	Jan.	8	−3150	−393.7

Number of options tested: 15
Total profits: −$2,765
Average number of trades per option: 6.27
Average profit per option: −$184.3
T-statistic: −0.212

A MEDIOCRE TRADING METHOD

Only four methods performed with mixed results, and none performed poorly. One of the so-so's—the 29-day trading method (Trading Method 7-7)—is presented.

8

Price Objectives

THE PRICE OBJECTIVE METHOD

Trend methods are sometimes regarded as quite good for entering a position, but only so-so for exiting. Often by the time a moving average or other method gets out of a trade position, the trend is not only over, but a reversal has eroded away a large portion of the potential profits. For example, for a Moving Average Method to exit a position near or at the top of a trend, the price would be required to maintain itself at its most favorable level long enough for the longer moving average to reach this level, and then move slightly and slowly in the opposite direction so that the short moving average could cross the long moving one near the most favorable level. Rarely does this happen, however. Usually, after reaching a peak, the price begins reversing its direction, if only temporarily, causing the shorter moving average to cross the longer at a level far below the top of the trend (if the position were long) or the bottom of a trend (if the position were short). A similar problem can be seen for Price Channel Trading Methods.

Analysts have attempted to set rules to remedy this condition, either by divorcing those rules for exiting a trade from those for entry, or by creating rules that under special conditions precede the method rules for exiting.

Special precedence rules would be especially useful when the trend develops very rapidly. The greater an advance in a flurry of speculation, the more likely second thoughts will cause the price to drop rapidly. In these cases a trending method will lose most of the price movement before a method signal indicates an exit from the trade.

The rule tested here is simple, and its success would indicate that more sophisticated rules might prove even more profitable. The rule states that if during a trade the price at any time moves favorably a predetermined number of points, the trade is exited with that profit. Let's illustrate this. A long position is entered at 155.60 in New York silver, and the predetermined price objective is 500 points. If a sell signal is indicated by the Closing Price Channel or Moving Average Method before the price ever touches 160.60 (500 points), the long position is liquidated and a short position initiated. However, if before such a signal is indicated the price touches 160.60, the position is then liquidated and short position is initiated only when the basic trading method so determines.

Conversely, a short position is entered at 155.60, with the same predetermined price objective. If the price moves as low as 150.60 before a long position is signaled, the position is liquidated then, a long position not entered until so indicated by the trading method. If the price does not drop that far, the usual reversal signal is precedent.

This Price Objective Method, like the Protective Stop Method discussed in the next chapter, is predicated on an assumption regarding the underlying behavior of silver price movements. A price objective asserts that a trend has a tendency to "tire." Once it has moved so far in one direction, it will tend to stop or reverse rather than continue. This is a statement on the activity of speculators. If price objectives are successful, then speculators will only ride a trend so far before, on average, more people profit by exiting the market than new speculators join the trend by acting late on the information that had attracted the earlier comers. Additionally, those speculators that were in the position incorrectly in the first place will take only so much of a loss before liquidating. Remember that each open contract requires a short and a long—a promise to deliver the commodity and a promise to receive it. As the price moves in one direction, say upward, those willing to take delivery at that price become fewer, and those willing to deliver at that

98

price becomes greater. Bidding for the silver will decline, and the price will no longer rise. Bidding to deliver the silver will increase, and the price will decline.

Although this price theoretical description is correct, it does not necessarily follow that price objectives increase profits. Only the computer can confirm or reject this hypothesis. Objectives exist. A price objective is a statement on the average reaction of speculators to a concerted price trend. But concerted trends can occur for a number of reasons. One is pure speculative activity without any substantial economic reason—follow-the-leader types, for instance—some begin buying, others follow. How far the price trends depends greatly on the number of speculators interested in silver at the moment, their positions, and the price level at the beginning of the trend. For an upward trend, the lower the initial price, the higher it is likely to go before resistance sets in.

Price trends in silver are also responses to international monetary and domestic fiscal policies. These vary so much that economic responses to them will cause price trends of widely differing amounts and velocity. So, it's impossible to choose *a* price movement at which speculators tire. An objective is *only* an average reaction. These objections notwithstanding, if the average length of concerted trends before adjustment are not so variant that immense profits will be missed, then an objective can improve on the basic method. A truly sophisticated method, however, will not be based on a single amount, but rather itself will be a function of volatility, previous price movements, and econometric information largely regarding the money supply. Such a method would also include measurements of speculative interest, using primarily volume of sales of futures contracts and open interest as the measurements.

Admitting the naïveté of using the single number price objective as a tool, the computer test yielded gratifying results. Five predetermined objectives were tested—1000 points, 1250 points, 1500 points, 1750 points, and 2000 points. Each of the four accepted trading methods were tested over all 15 options. The language used was as before, as was the computer. The operating system was Calidoscope.

Historically, price objectives on silver futures have proved effective. Of all four trading methods, *only price objectives increase the profits of the basic trading method without sacrificing any other quality.* Yet these price objectives are not different for each trading method, which lends credence to the view that, on average, defining the trend in four different manners, when a trend begins resistance, builds up as it continues, and that this resistance ends the trends. Objectives in the 1500 point to 2000 point range seem to work best. There is some indication that objectives greater than 2000 points would be effective, but testing of price objectives greater than 2000 points has not yet been done by the authors. Chart 8-1 below lists each method and price objective, with a W indicating when the objective decreases profits, and a B when the objective increases profits.

Chart 8-1

Method	1000 point	1250 point	1500 point	1750 point	2000 point
Moving Average 25-8	W	W	W	B	B
Closing Price Channel 9	W	B	B	B	B
Closing Price Channel 21	B	B	B	B	B
Closing Price Channel 13	W	B	B	B	B

The 1750- and 2000-point price objectives improve the profits of the basic trading method in all cases. The 1250- and 1500-point objectives improve profits on each Closing Price Channel Method, and they decrease profits only with the Moving Average Method. Finally, the 1000-point objective increases profits only with the 21-day Closing Price Channel Method.

Apparently the 25- and 8-day Moving Average Method is less responsive than price channels to improvement by price objectives. On the one hand, the 2000-point objective improves the 25- and 8-day Moving Average Method the most, increasing profits from about $39,000 to $50,000—a 30-percent increase. On the other hand, the 9-day closing price channel is improved 43 percent by the 1750-point price objective, the 21-day 38 percent by the 1500-point objective, and the 13-day 40 percent by the 2000 pointer. A conjecture that since the moving average gets in and out of trades faster than the closing price channels, price objectives work less well because reversal signals occur too soon in the trend is hardly valid.

The 25- and 8-day Moving Average Method had a mean trades per option of 9.27. Only the 21-day closing price channel had fewer —7.53. The 13-day averaged 13.47 trades per option, while the rapid 9-day channel averaged 21.33 trades per option. The solidest conclusion on the poorer performance Moving Average Method with price objectives is that it enters a trend and leaves the reversal later than does a closing price method. This is supported by the 38-percent improvement of the 21-day, the lowest of the three price channels, and the method certain to enter a trend later than the other two. Further, the 21-day Closing Price Channel Method was improved most by the 1500-point objective, while the other two channel methods were improved by most larger price objectives.

The 2000-point objective, from analyzing the historical record, should be used in conjunction with the 25- and 8-day Moving Aver--age Cross-over Method. Not only did profits increase 30 percent, in itself worthwhile, but the one losing option was only $40, lowering the reserve requirements. Additionally, two options lost with the basic method, while only one, the above, lost with the 2000-point objective. The December 1968 option, which lost $985 without objectives, profited 2785 with the 2000 pointer. Certainly the t-statistic is larger.

The 9-day price channel should be used with a 1750-point objective. No option lost, while another without an objective did. The improvement by this objective is consistent. Only two of the 15 options tested performed more poorly with the objective than without, while one performed identically, and 12 performed better.

Although the 1500-and 1750-point objectives produced more profits than the 2000-point one when used with the 21-day price channel, the last is preferable. The 1500-point objective loses in three options, the greatest loss being $1570, far above the $1000 limit. The 1750-point objective loses in only one option, but this loss is $1070, over the limit. The 2000-point objective loses in one option, and this is only $750. Its advantage is that its reserve requirements will outweigh the others' advantage in profits.

Lastly, the 13-day closing price channel should be used with a 1750-point objective, for reasons similar to the objective choice of the 21-day closing price channel. The 2000-point objective, with slightly higher overall profits, loses in two options, while the 1750 pointer loses in none.

9

Protective Stops

ADDING TO THE METHODS

If, after extensive testing, the methods endorsed in this book seem to work, a speculator will no doubt try to modify and improve them. This should not be attempted, of course, without testing over a large number of silver futures options.

The speculator will wonder frequently if there are ways of testing for the likelihood of a particular trade performing poorly. Perhaps there is a certain technique in inspecting the behavior either immediately before or after an execution signal that gives some estimation of a trade's success. Sometimes the trade will never be ahead, but immediately after the price enters, it will move adversely into a whipsaw. The search for an early exit from such trades is universal among commodity speculators, with those in silver even more zealous. There seems to be no end to price behavior that generates sophisticated approaches in trading methods. If the price moves beneficially and suddenly turns adversely, some speculators advocate immediate exit.

A much publicized addition to any basic trading method is the *protective stop*. This is said to prevent whipsaws by accepting a small loss on a trade rather than waiting for a beneficial reversal that may lead into much larger losses. A protective stop means that if a trade is entered and the price moves adversely by at least a certain amount—an amount sufficiently large to spark irregular fluctuations—then the trade should be exited. This protective stop is based on the same fundamental principle as the basic method itself—autocorrelation in price movements.

The assumption of the protective stop is as follows. Although the basic closing price channel or moving average attempts to isolate trends from temporary and irregular fluctuations, it can err by signaling a nonexistent trend. Since autocorrelation suggests that under some conditions a price moving in one direction will tend to continue in that direction, an adverse move will more likely continue than abate. These, then, are some reasons why certain speculators champion protective stops.

Whether or not this is true, only testing over a long period can tell. A sharper definition of a protective stop is this: If a trade is entered and the price moves adversely by a predetermined amount at any time during the trade before the regular exit signal, the trade should be exited immediately. Suppose that predetermined amount were 100 points, and a silver contract is sold short at 155.60. If the price immediately moves to 156.60, the trade is exited at that point, and a $100 loss is accepted. This doesn't mean that a contract is entered long at 156.60. Not a rule for entering a position, a protective stop is an ancillary rule for exiting in conjunction with the basics of the trading method. Under a sufficiently large adverse price movement, the protective stop's rule on exiting takes precedence over the basic trading method's for exiting. If a position is exited through a protective stop, a new position is not entered until signaled by the basic trading method. For example, if a long trade is entered and exited via a protective stop, then the next trade will be a short position when signaled with the basic trading method.

The size of the stop is crucial, of course. If it is too close to the price at which a trade is entered, fluctuations will saddle the trade with small losses. On the one hand, constant small fluctuations must be expected, and at the beginning of a trade they will frequently set it back temporarily. On the other hand, too large a stop will have little if any effect, thereby defeating the purpose of a protective stop, or it will saddle the trading with very large losses that could have been avoided, in part, had the trade remained open. Only testing can decide what protective stop is too small or too large.

The computer test was used on every trading method that the

original tests were performed on, and the results for the four accepted methods are presented below. Fifty-, 100-, 150-, 200-, and 250-point stops were tested on each of the trading methods over 15 options.

TRADING METHOD 9-1

Results of 9-Day Closing Price Channel Trading Method With Protective Stops

Year	Option	No Stop	50 Points	100 Points	150 Points	200 Points	250 Points
1968	July	4160	2050	1400	2670	2120	1570
1969	July	4525	3065	2115	2475	1805	1005
1970	July	1140	10	−670	−110	740	2460
1971	July	1860	1300	150	−1000	−2050	−3100
1967	Dec.	7925	4240	5100	8075	8025	7975
1968	Dec.	7710	4715	3865	3695	4040	3290
1969	Dec.	1815	−615	−1715	−2815	−3865	−505
1970	Dec.	6380	2930	4210	4730	4440	5510
1971	Dec.	1645	155	−645	−935	−515	−1215
1968	Sept.	6830	5550	5000	4450	4300	3800
1969	Sept.	4125	2865	1915	965	1965	1545
1970	Sept.	1040	1900	890	1500	2450	3610
1971	Sept.	−690	−1230	−2070	−3160	−2620	−1420
1970	May	2695	−655	2255	2475	1975	3435
1972	Jan.	1395	−985	−1405	−1885	−255	−905
Totals		52555	25295	20395	21190	22555	27055
T-statistics			2.4	1.8	1.6	3.2	2.5

105

TRADING METHOD 9-2

Results of 13-Day Closing Price Channel Trading Method
With Protective Stops

Year	Option	No Stop	50 Points	100 Points	150 Points	200 Points	250 Points
1968	July	4420	−855	−1305	−1755	3450	2570
1969	July	3150	−1330	−2030	−2730	−3430	−4730
1970	July	1740	790	−60	790	−270	−170
1971	July	5680	2390	1790	4910	6230	5840
1967	Dec.	5025	3090	2980	3805	5606	5555
1968	Dec.	1180	2505	3905	3305	2705	2105
1969	Dec.	1360	−1520	−2320	−3120	−2380	−1340
1970	Dec.	4490	−680	−1330	−1510	−2110	2370
1971	Dec.	1830	160	2080	1660	2040	3250
1968	Sept.	1415	−1140	4625	4125	3625	3125
1969	Sept.	1112	−1520	−2320	−3120	−3920	−4720
1970	Sept.	5120	1250	600	1660	1060	2960
1971	Sept.	3725	−905	−385	625	795	295
1970	May	1775	−855	−1305	−1755	−505	−345
1972	Jan.	955	895	755	255	1795	1395
Totals		42977	2275	5680	7145	14690	18160

TRADING METHOD 9-3

Results of 21-Day Closing Price Channel Trading Method
With Protective Stops

Year	Option	No Stop	50 Points	100 Points	150 Points	200 Points	250 Points
1968	July	950	−1940	−2190	−2440	−1940	−2140
1969	July	−235	−855	2075	1675	2545	2195
1970	July	4515	−655	−1015	−1365	−1715	−2065
1971	July	3945	825	525	225	565	3915
1967	Dec.	2110	555	3630	3420	3275	3125
1968	Dec.	725	−760	−1160	−830	−1180	5145
1969	Dec.	2395	3415	3115	2815	2515	2215
1970	Dec.	3180	540	190	−160	−510	−860
1971	Dec.	−185	−855	−1015	−475	−1055	−695
1968	Sept.	3755	210	3425	3225	3025	2825
1969	Sept.	3420	3500	3250	3000	2750	6720
1970	Sept.	4310	−230	400	100	−100	−350
1971	Sept.	165	465	15	−155	645	395
1970	May	4675	3885	3785	3685	3585	3485
1972	Jan.	−600	−490	−840	−220	−750	−540
Totals		33065	7600	14190	12500	11655	23370

TRADING METHOD 9-4

Results of 25- and 8-Day Moving Average Trading Method
With Protective Stops

Year	Option	No Stop	50 Points	100 Points	150 Points	200 Points	250 Points
1968	July	5945	1335	5435	5185	5335	5765
1969	July	6350	−950	−1450	−1950	−580	−1030
1970	July	2930	−760	−1160	−1560	−2070	−2420
1971	July	−690	−950	300	−100	−80	−320
1967	Dec.	4225	2955	3115	2985	7225	7125
1968	Dec.	−985	−1045	−1595	−2145	−2695	−3245
1969	Dec.	4485	−1045	265	−235	−735	−1235
1970	Dec.	3385	−255	−655	785	485	185
1971	Dec.	1285	−855	2245	2315	2065	1815
1968	Sept.	1070	−760	−1160	−1560	−1960	−2360
1969	Sept.	3070	−1140	−1740	−2340	−1060	−1610
1970	Sept.	3225	365	−35	−435	−835	−1235
1971	Sept.	150	−1140	1940	1810	1410	1080
1970	May	3060	−760	−1160	−1550	−1900	−2250
1972	Jan.	1180	1030	2130	2210	1960	1710
Totals		38685	−3975	6475	3415	6565	1975

COMPUTER RESULTS

The computer tests showed protective stops to be failures when used with the otherwise successful trading methods. No protective stop performed well on *any* of the trading methods. In the silver market 50 points is a very small amount, and fluctuations of this size occur constantly. Consequently, the 50-point stop performed the worse overall. Larger protective stops performed better, but none approached the level of profits attained from the basic methods. Apparently, the "experts," many of whom have advocated protective stops without testing them, were wrong again. Their theory seemed plausible; however, testing shows that when a successful trending method signals a trend, the tendency is in that direction despite substantial adverse movements. Test results indicate that no matter how adverse the price movement in a particular trade, the probability is that it will reverse itself rather than continue adversely. This was substantiated by the results of the protective stop tests on the other successful trading methods.

Protective stops improved poorly performing trending methods. Although not shown here, the stops reduced very large losses to moderate ones and even improved some moving average methods sufficiently to yield small profits. Apparently the theory on protective stops has some validity even though the methods themselves are not so compatible. In these cases, trend signals do not display strong underlying trends in the market.

Not all stops will perform as poorly as protective stops, however. Stops based on the behavior of the data should perform better than those based on a particular number of points, whether or not the market is volatile or sluggish. Some tests we conducted on other kinds of stops showed great promise. For example, more popular than the protective stop is the *trailing stop*—this changes with the prices and follows them during a period of profits. The trailing stop might move by a trend line or a moving average, or the current price during a trade less a particular amount. These stops might prove to be much more successful. However, there's no evidence that protective stops with these methods are profitable tools in the silver market. They may prove to be disastrous.

10

Statistical Tools

USING THE T-STATISTIC

How does a speculator learn confidence in a trading method? We shall develop an intuitive approach to a formal statistical test that may be used as a confidence "yardstick." We shall see how the *t-statistic* satisfies all intuitive demands for a trading method in which to place our confidence.

Suppose three trading methods are tested—the first over a year, the second over two years, and the third over five—with the following profits:

Method 1	Method 2	Method 3
$435	$440	$246
	385	503
		405
		358
		505
Mean		
(Average) $435	$412.50	$403.40

Method 1 has a higher average profit than Method 2, which in turn has a higher average profit than Method 3. Yet, if a speculator had to choose a method for trading, he would undoubtedly

111

choose the third one. Obviously Method 3's most attractive feature is the length of time over which it has been tested. The results over a shorter period could be an exception to the general behavior of the method, but five consecutive years of profits suggests that the results are more representative of the method's long-term performance. The longer a method is tested with favorable results, the more confidence the speculator will have in it. This length of time is measured in options. An option's trading life is the unit in our development of a test of confidence. The number of options over which the trading method is tested will be called *N-options*. N for the first method is 1, for the second 2, and for the third 5.

Suppose three trading methods have each been tested the same number of options, with the following average profits per option:

Method 1	*Method 2*	*Method 3*
−$258	$129	$385

Method 1 would be rejected immediately. A method with an average loss is worthless no matter the length of time it has been tested. Given that Methods 2 and 3 had no information save their average profits per year and the retesting of an equal number of options, then Method 3 would be the choice because of its higher average profit, other qualities being equal.

The average of a test is $\bar{x}$—the accepted statistical notation. In a sample, each observation is called an x_i, with i representing the number of observations in the sample. In our testing, a sample is the performance of a trading method over a number of options. Each option is an observation in the sample.

Suppose Method 4 were tested over three options, with the following results:

Method 4

Option 1	$100 = x_1
Option 2	200 = x_2
Option 3	150 = x_3
Total	$450 = X

112

X is the notation for the sum of the observations—that is, the sum of the option profits of the trading method.

So, $X = x_1 + x_2 + \ldots + x_n$, where n, as shown before, represents the number of options tested, or the number of observations in a sample.

Applied to Method 4,

$$X = x_1 + x_2 + x_3$$

$$X = 100 + 200 + 150$$

$$X = 450$$

Now, as $\bar{x}$ represents the average profit per year, or the average of the sum of observations in a sample, $\bar{x}$ is the sum of the profits divided by the number of options tested.

In notation, $\bar{x} = X/N$

For Method 4, $\bar{x} = 450/3 = 150$, as is already known.

Here are three examples to review the concepts we've introduced.

Example 1

A trading method was tested over a four-option period with the following results for each option.

Option	Profit
1	$100
2	200
3	100
4	100

Find N, all the x_i's, X, and $\bar{x}$.

N = the number of observations = the number of options tested
= 4

$x_1 = 100$ = the first observation = the first option's results.

$x_2 = 200$ = the second observation = the second option's results

$x_3 = 100$ = the third observation = the third option's results

$x_4 = 100 =$ the fourth observation = the fourth option's results

$X = x_1 + x_2 + x_3 + x_4 = 500$

$\bar{x} = X/N = 500/4 = 125$

Example 2

If $\bar{x} = 200$ and $N=5$, what is X, since $\bar{x} = X/N$, $200 = X/5$, and $X = 1000$

$\sum$ means summation. We shall use this symbol in place of

$x_1 + x_2 + x_3 \ldots \ldots + x_n$.   Then $X = \sum_{i=1}^{n} x_i$

i is called an index. It indicates the observation in the sample and means that the summing is from the first observation to the Nth.

Thus $\sum_{i=1}^{n} x_1 = x_1 + x_2 + x_3 + x_4$ when referring to

Method 4, and $\sum_{i=1}^{n} x_1 = x_1 + x_2 + \ldots + x_n$, where N is the number of observations, or, in this case, the number of options tested on a trading method.

With this stated, it follows that X, the total profits summed over all the options tested, equals $\sum_{i=1}^{n} x_i$,

where each x_i is one tested option. So far, the number of options tested and the average profits per option are the two indicators of confidence developed. Now, let's consider a third one.

Example 3

Again, following the hypothetical results of two trading methods:

Option	Method 1	Method 2
1	$100	$700
2	300	- 300
3	150	- 200
4	250	600
	X = $800	X = $800
$\bar{x} = X/N =$	$200	$200

Methods 1 and 2 have been tested with the same number of options, each showing the same average profit. Which should you choose? With few exceptions, your choice should be Method 1.

Method 1's consistency makes it preferable to Method 2. Method 1 shows a profit each option, with the range between the best and worst results being only $200. Method 2 shows a profit in two options, and a loss in two options; the range between the best and worst options is $1,000, five times as large. Confidence in Method 2 is undermined by its wild fluctuations. On the one hand, one intuitively is hardly confident that this average result over four options represents the method's long-run behavior. On the other hand, Method 1's regular behavior gives the impression that the sample better represents its long-run behavior.

MEASURING CONSISTENCY

How, then, should consistency be measured? One way is by looking at a sample's range. Method 1 has a range of $200, and Method 2 a range of $1,000. But a sample's range has two serious shortcomings: it can be affected too much by an unusual option; its consistency is measured by only two observations from the sample itself.

Here's an example of these shortcomings.

Option		Method 1	Method 2
1		200	600
2		-700	-500
3		600	-300
4		400	800
5		500	800
6		600	-100
7		500	800
	X	2100	2100
	x̄	300	300
	Range	1300	1300

In this test, Methods 1 and 2 not only have been tested over the same number of options, but both have identical average profits per option as well as identical ranges. Yet Method 1 is preferable although it carries the largest single loss in any given option—$700 in option 2. Except for that loss, each option showed consistent and profitable results. Method 2, conversely, carries the single largest profit in any option—$800—three times, but losses in three options, while Method 1 has only one loss. The range has clearly failed to discriminate between two methods, one of which is intuitively more desirable than the other. The difference in this case depends not on the best and worst results, which Method 2 has, but on the intermediate results.

So, a suitable measure of consistency, or variability of a sample, must involve each option in that sample. Noteworthy is that much of a method's sample of option profits will involve the results of each option and observation.

MEASURING A SAMPLE'S VARIABILITY

Measurement of a sample's variability requires a standard. This standard must be such that if all components of the sample are identical, the measure of variability will be 0. Obviously the greater the variability of the members of the sample, then the greater will be the measure. This standard is the sample average, $\bar{x}$. In statistics, the common average is called the sample mean, a notation followed throughout this chapter. So, $\bar{x}$ is the *mean*. The mean is the best standard because the greater the variability of the observations, the greater will be the distances of each observation from the mean. No other standard always has this property.

How should the deviation from the mean be used as a measure of variability? One way is by subtracting the mean from each observation; in this case, mean profits from each option's profits, as follows:

Option	Method 2	Deviation $(x_i - \bar{x})$	
1	600	600–300	300
2	−500	−500–300	−800
3	−300	−300–300	−600
4	800	800–300	500
5	800	800–300	500
6	−100	−100–300	−400
7	800	800–300	500
X	2100	Sum of Deviation	0
$\bar{x}$	300		

Here's the error in measuring the variability by summing the deviation of each option's profits from the mean option profits. The result must be 0. For every amount over the mean of the sample, there must be an amount under it. The mean is that point that is the sample's "center of gravity." Thus, the sum of deviations between each option and the mean of all the options cannot be used.

Refer once again to the result of Method 2.

Option	Profit	Deviation	Square of Deviation
1	600	300	90000
2	−500	−800	640000
3	−300	−600	360000
4	800	500	250000
5	800	500	250000
6	−100	−400	160000
7	800	500	250000

Sum of squares of deviations   2000000

$$= \sum_{i=1}^{n} (x_i - \bar{x})^2$$
$$= (x_1 - \bar{x})^2 + (x_2 - \bar{x})^2 + \ldots + (x_7 - \bar{x})^2$$
$$= (600-300)^2 + (-500-300)^2 + \ldots + (800 - 300)^2$$
$$= 300^2 + (-800)^2 + \ldots + 500^2$$
$$= 2000000$$

117

For most applications in statistics, the sum of squares of the deviations between the observations and the sample mean is used as the basis of a measure of variability. Recalling that the square of a number is that number multiplied by itself, we denote the square of a number x by x^2. x^2 = x times x. 5^2 = 5 squared = 5 x 5 = 25.

The sum of squares of deviations do not add to 0 because the squares of negative numbers are positive, as any two negative numbers multiplied yield a positive result. The process of calculating the sum of squares of deviations of the observations of a sample from the sample mean will be presented in a simpler example.

Given the sample

6
8
3
4
9

First, $X = \sum\limits_{i=1}^{n} x_i$ is calculated.

$x_1 = 6; x_2 = 8; x_3 = 3; x_4 = 4; x_5 = 9$

$X = \sum\limits_{i=1}^{5} x_1 = 6 + 8 + 3 + 4 + 9 = 30$

Second, $\bar{x}$ is calculated.

$\bar{x} = X/N = 30/5 = 6.0$

Third, the deviations $(x_1 - \bar{x})$ are calculated.

x_i	$\bar{x}$	$x_i - \bar{x}$
6	6	0
8	6	2
3	6	-3
4	6	-2
9	6	3

Forth, the deviations are squared.

Deviation	*Deviation^2*
0	0
2	4
-3	9
-2	4
3	9

Fifth, the squares of deviations are summed.

Returning to Method 2, the sum of squares is found to be 2,000,000. The sum of squares (named SSD) by itself cannot be used as a good measure of variability. Suppose, for example, that Method 2 was tested 14 options instead of 7, and that the last 7 performed identically to the first set. The SSD would be exactly twice as large. But the sample is no less consistent. In fact, more confidence can be placed in the 14 sample tests than the 7, as the test occurred during a longer period with identical consistency and mean profit.

The measure of variability desired, then, should not depend on the number of observations in the sample, or the number of silver options over which a trading method is tested. It should be sample-size invariant, so that the variability of samples of differing sizes can be compared. This does not mean the size of the sample does not matter, only that a measure of confidence includes descriptions of a sample of trading methods which do not depend on sample size. Obviously to satisfy this requirement the SSD should be divided by N, the sample size, to modify the measure of variability into constant units.

SQUARE DEVIATIONS

SSD/N is known as the variance of a sample, and it is denoted by s^2 also called the *mean square deviation*.

$$\text{Thus } s^2 = SSD/N = \sum_{i=1}^{n} \frac{(x_i - \bar{x})^2}{N}$$

For fairly technical reasons, in practical statistics SSD is usually divided by N-1. SSD/N-1 is called the estimate of the sample variance. This causes the variance to be slightly larger than otherwise. Justification is based on the fact that in any sample of a theoretically larger population, the chances are that a very extreme observation was excluded from the sample, and so the sample estimate tends to underestimate the population variance.

$$\text{Henceforth, } s^2 = SSD \ / \ (N - 1) = \sum_{i=1}^{n} \frac{(x_i - \bar{x})^2}{N-1}$$

For Method 2, SSD = 2,000,000 / (7 - 1) = 333,333

Associated with the statistic s^2 is the statistic s. $s/^2$ is the measure of the mean square deviation, while for confidence tests the square root of the variance is desired, as it is in the same units as the mean and observations.

$$s = \sqrt{s^2}$$

The square root of a number is the operation inverse to the square of a number. The square root of a number x is another number y, such that $y^2 = x$.

Thus, $\sqrt{25} = 5$,
as 5 times 5 is 25

$$\text{Then } s = \sqrt{s^2} = \sqrt{\frac{SSD}{N-1}} = \frac{\sqrt{SSD}}{\sqrt{N-1}}$$

For Method 2,

$$s = \sqrt{s^2} \quad = \quad \sqrt{333,333} \quad = \quad 577.4$$

The method of calculating square roots should be familiar to most readers. For those who have forgotten, the operation is available in most high school math books.

s is known most commonly as the *standard deviation* and occasionally as the *root mean square deviation*.

It is impossible in such short space to give a complete treatment of the development of the "right" tests of confidence. But our primary interest here is the presentation of trading methods, leaving little space for statistical discussion. We shall attempt to convince you that an objective and intuitively acceptable measure exists. If you are unfamiliar with statistical tests of hypotheses, but have an interest in understanding more fully the arguments developed here, we suggest you consult a basic statistics book for a few nights' study. It may be surprising how logically and convincingly statistical tools are developed and presented. Unlike many other fields of mathematics, statistics is empirical development.

The first interest in probability theory was in regard to gambling, and most recently statistical theory was motivated by the need to test hypotheses in problems in psychology, medicine, and business. More sophisticated tools than are presented here control quality in production, insure the effectiveness of medicines, even determine a department store's inventory. With apologies extended, our treatment is somewhat sketchy, but we believe it is sufficient to offer an intuitive basis for confidence in any of the trading methods treated in later chapters.

AN INTUITIVE BASIS

The profits of each option tested on a specific trading method can be thought of as the *value* of that option. If the trading method is tested over several or many options, the values have a distribution, ranging from the option with the highest profits to that with the lowest (or the greatest loss). The rest of the values vary in size between these two extremes. Suppose it were desired to graph the values of the options to get an idea of the frequency with which the options acquired different-sized values—the amount of profits. To get a sharper picture, it might be desired to divide the values into classes over a range of values so that, say, $455 and $460 would fall in the same class. A graph done in this manner is a *frequency distribution*. Refer to Chart 10-1.

CHART 10-1

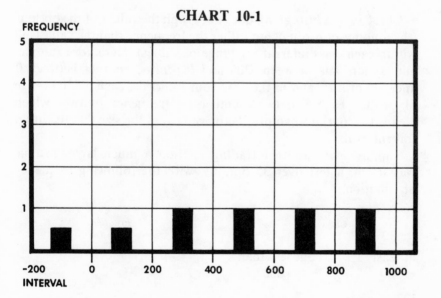

Option	Profits	
1	500	
2	375	
3	-200	Each range of values is a *class interval.*
4	900	Here, a class interval of 200 seems as
5	750	good as any—not breaking the values into
6	285	so many classes that each option is in
7	680	a different class, but not lumping them
8	550	all together.
9	125	
10	890	

Class Size: 200	*Qualifying Options (Tally)*	
Class 1: -200 to 0	#3	1
Class 2: 0 to 200	#9	1
Class 3: 200 to 400	#2, #6	2
Class 4: 400 to 600	#1, #8	2
Class 5: 600 to 800	#10, #4	2

Chart 10-1, a *histogram,* does not graph the values of the options (the amount of profits), but rather the frequency that the values fell within each class interval (or range of values). Here, for example, one option was between -200 and 0 profits, another between 0 and 200 profits, and in the next four intervals, each a $200 range of profits, each had two members, a frequency of two, which means two options had profits (or values) of the size that fit within this interval.

Suppose with another trading method a much larger sample was taken, a test over 35 options, with the following frequency distribution.

Class Size		Frequency
at least	but less than	
-500	-300	2

-300	-100	1
-100	100	3
100	300	4
300	500	7
500	700	8
700	900	5
900	1100	3
1100	1300	1
1300	1500	1

SEEKING A NORMAL DISTRIBUTION

These are plotted on Chart 10-2. Notice that unlike the frequency distribution in Chart 10-1, most of the options bulged in the middle-class intervals, and toward the more extreme values (profits and losses) fewer options occur. This is common in large samples drawn from experiments in biology, economics, chemistry, and physics. Very large samples, when plotted in a histogram, begin to bulge in the center, then decline toward the edges, much like a bell-shaped curve. Most readers have seen the famous bell-shaped

CHART 10-2

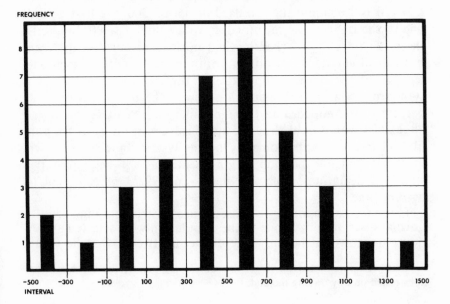

curve, describing the distribution of intelligence quotients, family incomes, heights of males from 25 to 29 years of age, and so forth. This curve is *a normal distribution.* A normal distribution is only theoretical and assumes an infinite population from which a sample is drawn. But even though theoretical, it is a model describing almost all large sets of data. So the particular features of normal distributions are used to predict or estimate about a large population taken from a sample. A speculator might theorize, for example, that his historical test of a trading method on several options is drawn from a theoretically infinite population of options whose values (profits and losses) are normally distributed. That is, if all options were traded for a thousand years with any particular trading method, their profits would be a bell-shaped curve—approximately normal.

Chart 10-3 shows a normal distribution. Operating on the assumption that any test is drawn from an approximately normal distribution that the confidence test is based,* its histogram will look more like a normal distribution. The vertical line in this chart with the base value of 0 is the mean of the population. Those vertical lines marked with integral numbers are units of standard deviation of the population. That is, vertical 1 is one standard deviation above the mean. If the mean of a population normally distributed is 1,000 and the standard deviation 300, the first vertical line to the right of the mean will have a value of 1,300. Similarly, the other lines are marked by their positive or negative distances in units of standard deviations from the mean. Often the characteristics of the normal population is that within a distance of a standard deviation (plus or minus) from the mean will be 68.27 percent of the population. If the population had 1,000 members, about 683 would be within one standard deviation from the population mean, if approximately normally distributed. As shown, 95.45 percent of the population members will be within two standard deviations from the mean and 99.73 percent will be within three.

This fact has significant consequences when sampling from a normal distribution. If one of the population were selected at random, there would be only one chance in twenty that he would

*This presupposes that the larger the sample, the greater the number of options tested on any trading method.

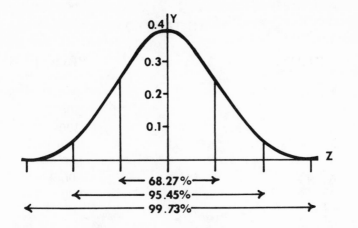

be more than two standard deviations from the mean, one chance in 400 that he would be more than three deviations, and slightly more than three chances in ten of being more than one.

This leads to the test statistic t. t is defined as $\dfrac{\bar{x} - M_O}{s / \sqrt{N}}$

M_O, known as the test hypothesis, is a number. This statistic tests the probability that if M_O were really the population mean from which the sample being tested were drawn, $\bar{x}$ could occur as the sample mean. In other words, it tests the probability that the difference between the hypothetical population mean and the sample mean would occur if the sample were drawn at random. It so happens that for large samples, N greater than or equal to 30, the t statistic is approximately normally distributed, and the estimates could be taken from the normal distribution. But the estimating is not good for samples under 30, and a T distribution has been calculated for each N. Now the t statistic has a mean of 0 and a standard deviation of 1.

To demonstrate these concepts more clearly, let's apply them to Method 2 again (see Chart 10-4). Notice that the t statistic is calculated, and has a value of 1.37. What does this mean when the t distribution has a mean of 0 and a standard deviation of 1? In Chart 10-4 the test hypothesis is that the mean of the population from which the sample was drawn (the options on which the trading method was tested) is 0. This hypothesis conjectures the true per-

125

CHART 10-4

METHOD 2

OPTION	PROFIT
1	600
2	-500
3	-300
4	800
5	800
6	-100
7	800

$\bar{x} = 300$

$s = 577.4$

$\bar{x} + s = 877.4$

$\bar{x} - s = -277.4$

$$t = \frac{\bar{x} - 0}{s\sqrt{N}} = \frac{\bar{x}\sqrt{N}}{s}$$

$$t = (300)(2.65)/577.4$$

$$t = 1.37$$

formance of the trading method over a much larger sample (theoretically an infinite sample, but a large finite sample will do) is no profits. The t statistic then measures the likelihood of the sample mean being what it is if the mean is in fact 0. If the probability is very low, the hypothesis that the mean is zero is rejected, and confidence can be placed in the trading method. When it is said the probability that the trading method is profitable in the long run is 99 percent, this means that if the long-run performance of the method were 0, there is only one chance in a hundred that a

126

random sample of this size would show results at least as profitable as those in the sample. In other words, the chances of this sample being a rare representative of a dissimilar population is so low, as to be, inconsequential.

If it is desired to test the hypothesis that a trading method is profitable in the long run (if the sample tested is profitable), the test hypothesis should be set at zero, and the T-statistic takes the form:

$$t = \frac{\bar{x}}{s/\sqrt{N}}$$

This t will have a mean of 0, and a standard deviation of 1. In repeated sampling of size N, and with a test hypothesis of 0, the means of the sample would be distributed around 0 in such a manner that the mean of the sample means would be 0, and the standard deviation of the sample means would be 1.

Here's what the t of 1.37 in Method 2 means. If the mean of the larger population were 0, the chance of a single sample showing a mean of 300 would be the portion of samples that would occur in the distribution greater than 1.37 times the t-standard of 1.

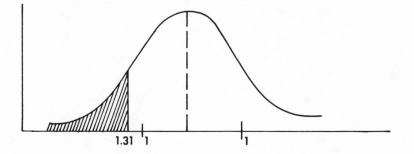

1.31   1   1

As the above figure indicates, the portion of samples with a mean of 300 or more would occur in about 20 to 25 percent of the total. In this case confidence could not be placed in the trading method, as the chance of getting the results of the sample if the true mean were 0 is too large. In this book, the confidence limit of 99 percent will be required. The t statistic must be large enough so that if the true mean were 0, the chances of the profitable results obtained would be less than 1 percent in the sample tested—namely, the 15 silver options tested.

Recognizing the incompleteness of this explanation, we suggest that you consult any statistics textbook for more information on the t statistic. Also, many texts have t tables, which show the t statistic required for various levels of confidence. These requirements themselves depend on the size of the sample.

The denomination of the t statistic is known as the standard error of the means. Then,

$$\bar{x} = \frac{s}{\sqrt{N}}$$

As the standard deviation is the measure of a sample's variability, the standard error is the variability of the means of a sample. Distribution of means almost always approximates a bell-shaped curve even if the population from which the samples were drawn is not normally distributed. The t test using 0 as the hypothesis is, in essence, finding what portion of the means of repeated samples would be contained within certain distances from the hypothetical mean of 0 (in units of the standard error). This is why the sample mean is divided by the *standard error,* which we shall soon be using.

11

Trading Procedure:
Following the Methods

MONITORING THE METHODS

Since commodities prices move spectacularly and suddenly, the trader must know his day-to-day position in the market. Unlike stocks, commodity investments can take terrible beatings in a matter of minutes or be cleaned out in a day. The trading methods we have covered thus far require day-to-day calculating and updating. In heavy trading new instructions must be given nearly every day to the broker. If the trader is limited to trading only one contract or has several contracts riding on a single position, the paperwork involved is relatively simple. In this case, the trader can probably muddle through the required calculations and broker instructions, using only his memory and a scrap of paper.

There are three activities in technical trading which the trader must monitor with accurate and timely records. He must follow the method daily, watching for the signal to buy or sell. He must instruct the broker promptly and accurately. And, he must be aware of *his* financial position. We shall explore some simple ways of monitoring these activities.

MONITORING THE MOVING AVERAGE METHOD

The Moving Average Cross-over Method discussed in Chapter 5 requires that two moving averages be calculated each day—a long moving average and the shorter "cross-over" one. It will be remembered that the signal to buy is indicated when the shorter

129

moving average moves from below to above the long moving one, and the signal to sell is indicated when the shorter moving average penetrates the long moving one from above. These are shown as A (sell) and B (buy) in Charts 5-1 and 5-2.

A simpler way of monitoring the two averages is to keep daily records of changes in tabular form. An example of tabular monitoring of a 30- and 8-day moving average is in Table 11-1. The table has nine columns. The third column is the day's closing price. This price can be obtained from any daily newspaper that publishes commodities prices. Once actual trading begins, however, the closing price should be obtained each day from the broker as soon after closing in order to make the required calculations and instruct the broker before business opens for the next day. Don't count on being able to contact your broker the following morning in time for him to enter your order before the opening bell. This precaution is directed especially to West Coast traders, for the New York silver market opens at 6:15 AM, Pacific Standard Time. All is not lost, however, as the buy or sell order is not executed until after the opening. The method will still be approximated; a few points either way over time will not greatly affect it.

Column 5, labeled 30-day total, is the moving 30-day total of closing prices. For example, the 30-day total of prices on January 17 is 4532.40—the sum of closing prices from December 3 through January 17 inclusive (remember we're talking about trading, not calendar, days). Column 6 lists the moving 30-day average. This price is simply the 30-day total divided by 30. Continuing our previous example, the 30-day average on January 17 is 151.080, obtained by dividing 4532 by 30. The numbers in the 8-day total and 3-day average columns are obtained in a similar manner. Column 10 is a convenient place for the actual execution prices. Columns 2 and 4 contain xs. Their function is to isolate the series of closing prices that are contained in the 30- and 8-day totals of closing prices. It will be remembered from Chapter 5 that it's not necessary to add 30 numbers each day to get the 30-day total. Once the first 30 days have been totaled, it is necessary only to add the new day's closing price to the 30-day total, and subtract the closing price 31 days ago. This will yield the new 30-day total. Referring to the table again, the total on January 17, 4532.40, was obtained in two steps:

130

30-day total, January 14	4518.00
1) Add: Closing price, January 17	160.80
Subtotal	4678.80
2) Subtract: Closing price, December 2	-146.40
New 30-day total	4532.40

The function of the x in column 2 is to identify the 31st day which is being subtracted. The function of the x in column 4 is to identify the ninth day which is being subtracted from the 8-day total. The xs are markers to help the trader in his daily calculations. They can be important in preventing confusion to the trader in a hurry. Notice, for example, that the closing prices on December 1 and 2 and on December 3 and 6 were the same, a circumstance that might lead to mistakes in calculation. When computing the 30-day average, for example, an error on one day will be carried forward to the next day in the new total, thereby compounding the error. For this reason, it is necessary from time to time to retotal an entire series of closing prices to eliminate any errors that may have crept in. It is good practice to retotal the entire series whenever an execution to buy or sell is indicated to make sure that the signal is valid and not the result of faulty arithemetic.* For example, to be sure that the sell signal indicated on January 5 is valid, it is wise to re-add the 30-day series from November 22 through January 5, and the 8-day series from December 23 through January 5; and then repeating the 30-day average and 8-day average calculations to make sure they are the same as those made the first time.

Monitoring the 30-, 8-day Moving Average Cross-over Method is done simply by comparing the 8-day average to the 30-day one once the calculations are completed. Referring again to Table 11-1, we see that three signals are indicated between November

*You may now be toying with the idea of buying an adding machine. We strongly recommend it. Adding a long series of numbers by hand is tedious work, and one is never sure of the accuracy unless it is repeated two or three times. Anyone with enough assets to speculate in silver ought to set some dollars aside for an adding machine, or better still a calculator that multiplies and divides. New compact electronic models are surprisingly inexpensive, if you take time to shop around.

TABLE 11-1

December 1972 Silver, New York

30-, 8-Day Moving Average

Date 1971-72		Closing Price		30-Day Total	30-Day Average	8-Day Total	8-Day Average	Instruction to Broker	Actual Execution
11-1	x	138.50	x	4437.50	147.916	1130.80	141.350		
11-3	x	139.80	x	4421.00	147.366	1129.00	141.125		
11-4	x	139.00	x	4402.40	146.746	1125.40	140.675		
11-5	x	140.90	x	4387.70	146.256	1123.70	140.462		
11-8	x	142.20	x	4374.30	145.810	1121.70	140.212		
11-9	x	142.20	x	4360.50	145.350	1123.80	140.475		
11-10	x	141.10	x	4345.80	144.860	1124.00	140.500		
11-11	x	143.10	x	4334.90	144.496	1126.80	140.850		
11-12	x	142.50	x	4322.80	144.093	1130.80	141.350		
11-15	x	143.70	x	4312.70	143.756	1134.70	141.837		
11-16	x	143.20	x	4302.40	143.413	1138.90	142.362		
11-17	x	142.60	x	4291.80	143.060	1140.60	142.575		
11-18	x	141.50	x	4285.10	142.836	1139.90	142.487		
11-19	x	142.20	x	4281.00	142.700	1139.90	142.487		
11-22	x	142.50	x	4275.90	142.530	1141.30	142.662		
11-23	x	141.70	x	4269.30	142.310	1139.90	142.487		
11-24	x	141.80	x	4266.60	142.220	1139.20	142.400		
11-26	x	143.40	x	4267.50	142.250	1138.90	142.362		
11-29	x	143.80	x	4267.70	142.256	1139.50	142.437		
11-30	x	143.40	x	4267.30	142.243	1140.30	142.537		
12-1	x	146.40	x	4268.40	142.280	1145.20	143.150	Buy 2	143.00B

								Sell 2	150.50S
								Buy 2	154.70B
12-2	x	146.40	x	4268.10	142.270	1149.40	143.675		
12-3		148.40	x	4272.60	142.420	1155.30	144.412		
12-6		148.40	x	4279.40	142.646	1162.00	145.250		
12-7		148.80	x	4285.60	142.853	1169.00	146.125		
12-8		149.80	x	4292.80	143.093	1175.40	146.925		
12-9		151.40	x	4300.00	143.333	1183.00	147.875		
12-10		151.20	x	4311.10	143.703	1190.80	148.850		
12-13		149.80	x	4320.00	144.000	1194.20	149.275		
12-14		150.30	x	4330.00	144.333	1198.10	149.762		
12-15		150.70	x	4342.20	144.740	1200.40	150.050		
12-16		152.80	x	4355.20	145.173	1204.80	150.600		
12-17		152.20	x	4368.40	145.613	1208.20	151.025		
12-20		149.90	x	4377.40	145.913	1208.30	151.037		
12-21		149.10	x	4384.30	146.143	1206.00	150.750		
12-22		149.40	x	4391.50	146.383	1204.20	150.525		
12-23		149.70	x	4400.10	146.670	1204.10	150.512		
12-27		146.70	x	4403.70	146.790	1200.50	150.062		
12-28		144.30	x	4405.50	146.850	1194.10	149.262		
12-29		145.90	x	4407.70	146.923	1187.20	148.400		
12-30		145.60	x	4410.10	147.003	1180.60	147.575		
1-3		148.10	x	4415.60	147.186	1178.80	147.350		
1-4		150.40	x	4424.50	147.483	1180.10	147.512		
1-5		150.40	x	4432.70	147.756	1181.30	147.637		
1-6		153.50		4443.70	148.123	1184.90	148.112		
1-7		154.80		4456.80	148.560	1193.00	149.125		
1-10		157.00		4472.00	149.066	1205.70	150.712		
1-11		154.60		4483.20	149.440	1214.40	151.800		
1-12		155.90		4495.30	149.843	1224.70	153.087		
1-13		154.50		4506.40	150.213	1231.10	153.887		
1-14		158.00		4518.00	150.600	1238.70	154.837		
1-17		160.80		4532.40	151.080	1249.10	156.137		

133

1 and January 17.* The first occurs on November 22: the 8-day average became larger than the 30-day.** The broker is instructed to buy two contracts of December silver at the market the next day, November 23. (One contract offsets the old short position, and the other contract initiates a new long position.) The next day the broker informs the trader of his price; a notation of this price is then entered in Column 9, "Execution Price."

The next signal occurs on January 5, the 8-day average at that time going below the 30-day. The procedure is repeated, except the trader shorts two contracts at 150.50. One contract offsets his previous long, and the other initiates a short position. The trader now has a $704.50 profit on his offset position.

January 6, sell	150.50
November 23, buy	−143.00
Gain	7.50 points

750 points times $1/point = $750.00
Less commission −45.50
$704.50

The next signal occurs on January 7. Two contracts are purchased at 154.20, one a new long position, and one offsetting the short position held at 150.50. The trader has just experienced the classic "whipsaw." Only two days after nailing down a $704.50 profit, he loses $415.50.

January 10, buy	154.20
January 6, sell	−150.50
Loss	3.70 points

*We are assuming here that a short position is being carried on November 1, having been initiated some time back; December 1972 silver, New York, began on July 29, 1971. Calculations would have begun on that day; that is, the first closing price entered on July 29. The first 8-day total and average would have been on August 9, and the first 30-day total and average would have been on September 14.

**On a graph, the 8-day trend line would have penetrated the 30-day trend line. A visual aid is provided by circling the 8-day average on the upside whenever it penetrates the 30-day.

370 points times $1/point = $370.00
          Plus commission   45.50
                                   ——————
                                  $415.50

MONITORING THE EXTREME PRICE CHANNEL METHOD

The Extreme Price Channel Method, remember, requires the trader to keep track of a high and low price within a certain time period. The trader must keep trace of the waiting period as well. Table 11-2 is a tabularized format of the Extreme Price Channel Method, with a 5-day channel and 3-day waiting period. The high and low prices shown are those of the July 1972 option (New York), October 28, 1971, through January 25, 1972. Chart 6-2 is a bar chart of this same option and time period.

The trader records in columns 2 and 3 the day's high and low prices. In column 4 he pencils in the 5-day high price and in column 6 the 5-day low. In column 5, the "waiting-day" high is recorded, and in column 7 the "waiting-day" low. Columns 8 and 9 are for the changes in the instructions to the broker. Column 10 is for recording the actual execution price.

Assuming that we want to begin trading with the 5-day channel, 3-day waiting method on November 4, we accumulate the high and low price data for the past five days and enter them in the table. Having done this, we inspect the data for the 5-day channel high and low. We see that the high is 137.40 and the low is 133.80; we enter these items in the appropriate columns. Since November 4 is also the first day of the waiting period, we also enter 137.40 and 133.80 as our waiting-day high and low. The waiting-day high and low are the most significant in the table because they form the basis of our order to the broker. In this case, the order would be to buy one contract at 137.50. On November 5, the next day, we enter the new high and low prices and determine the new 5-day high and 5-day low as before. November 5 is the second waiting day for the 3-day wait, so the waiting-day high and low do not change. On November 8, the next trading day, we get an execution, so we immediately update our waiting-day high and low to correspond to the 5-day high and low. Since we are now long one contract, our order to the broker should be entered to sell two contracts, one new and one offset. At what price? Inspecting the waiting-day low on November 8, which we have just calculated, this order will

TABLE 11-2

July 1972 Silver, New York

5-, 3-Day Extreme Price Channel

1 Date 1971-72	2 High Price	3 Low Price	4 5-Day High	5 Waiting Day High (Basis Market Open)	6 5-Day Low	7 Waiting Day Low (Basis Market Open)	8 Instruction to Broker-Execute	9 At	10 Actual Execution
10-28	136.90	135.30	—		—				
10-29	137.40	135.80	—		—				
11-1	136.20	134.60	—		—				
11-3	136.00	133.80	—		—				
11-4	136.70	135.00	137.40	137.40	133.80	133.80	Buy 1	137.50	
11-5	137.20	134.80	137.40	137.40	133.80	133.80			
11-8	138.50	136.20	138.50	138.50	133.80	133.80	Sell 2	133.70	137.50B
11-9	138.90	138.10	138.90	138.50	133.80	133.80			
11-10	137.80	136.70	138.90	138.90	134.80	133.80			
11-11	139.60	137.80	139.60	138.90	134.80	133.80			
11-12	139.40	138.20	139.60	139.60	136.20	134.80	Sell 2	134.70	
11-15	140.00	137.60	140.00	139.60	136.70	134.80			
11-16	140.00	139.00	140.00	140.00	136.70	136.20	Sell 2	136.10	
11-17	138.90	138.20	140.00	140.00	137.60	136.70	Sell 2	136.60	
11-18	139.60	137.10	140.00	140.00	137.10	136.70			
11-19	138.10	137.10	140.00	140.00	137.10	136.70	Sell 2	137.50	
11-22	139.10	136.00	140.00	140.00	136.00	137.60	Buy 2	140.10	137.20S
11-23	138.80	137.50	139.60	140.00	136.00	136.00			
11-24	138.10	137.30	139.60	139.60	136.00	136.00			
11-26	139.60	137.50	139.60	140.90	136.00	136.00	Buy 2	139.70	139.80B
11-29	140.90	139.70	140.90	140.90	137.30	136.00	Sell 2	135.90	
11-30	140.20	139.30	140.90	140.90	137.30	136.00			
12-1	142.60	139.80	142.60	140.90	137.50	136.00			
12-2	142.70	141.70	142.70	142.60	137.50	137.30	Sell 2	137.20	
12-3	144.50	141.80	144.50		139.30	137.30			

Date									
12-6	146.50	143.80	146.50	142.70	139.30	137.50	Sell 2	137.40	
12-7	145.20	143.10	146.50	144.50	139.80	139.30	Sell 2	139.20	
12-8	145.70	144.60	146.50	146.50	141.70	139.30	Sell 2	139.70	
12-9	147.20	145.90	147.20	146.50	141.80	139.80	Sell 2	141.60	
12-10	147.40	146.10	147.40	146.50	143.10	141.80	Sell 2	141.70	
12-13	146.40	145.30	147.40	147.20	143.10	143.10	Sell 2	143.00	
12-14	147.80	145.90	147.80	147.40	144.60	143.10			
12-15	146.50	144.20	147.80	147.40	144.20	144.60			
12-16	148.70	147.50	148.70	147.80	144.20	144.20	Sell 2	144.50	
12-17	148.90	147.90	148.90	147.80	144.20	144.20	Sell 2	144.10	
12-20	149.40	145.50	149.40	148.70	144.20	144.20			
12-21	146.50	145.00	149.40	148.90	144.70	144.20			
12-22	145.70	144.70	149.40	149.40	144.70	144.20			
12-23	145.70	145.10	149.40	149.40	144.70	144.20			
12-27	145.00	142.60	149.40	149.40	142.60	142.60	Buy 2	149.50	144.10S
12-28	142.20	140.00	146.50	149.40	140.00	142.60			
12-29	142.80	141.00	145.00	146.50	140.00	142.60			
12-30	144.10	141.60	145.70	145.70	140.00	140.00			
1-3	146.50	142.20	146.50	145.70	141.00	140.00	Buy 2	146.60	
1-4	147.90	144.40	147.90	146.50	141.60	140.00	Buy 2	145.80	
1-5	149.30	146.00	149.30	147.90	142.20	140.00	Sell 2	139.90	145.80B
1-6	151.40	146.40	151.40	149.30	144.40	140.00			
1-7	152.80	148.40	152.80	151.40	146.00	141.00	Sell 2	140.90	
1-10	154.20	149.30	154.20	152.80	146.40	141.60	Sell 2	141.50	
1-11	151.80	149.80	154.20	154.20	148.40	142.20	Sell 2	142.10	
1-12	152.40	149.90	154.20	154.20	149.30	144.40	Sell 2	144.30	
1-13	154.20	149.30	154.20	154.20	149.30	146.00	Sell 2	145.90	
1-14	156.90	150.50	156.90	156.90	149.30	146.40	Sell 2	146.30	
1-17	156.10	155.30	156.90	156.90	149.30	148.40	Sell 2	148.30	
1-18	156.20	153.60	156.90	156.90	150.50	149.30	Sell 2	149.20	
1-19	154.90	153.50	156.90	156.90	151.50	149.30			
1-20	153.80	152.30	156.90	156.90	150.30	149.30			
1-21	153.70	151.50	156.20	156.20	149.30	149.30			
1-24	152.20	150.30	156.20			150.50	Sell 2	150.40	150.40S
1-25		149.30				149.30	Buy 2	156.30	

137

be at 133.70—that is, a ticket below the waiting-day low of 133.80. Notice the timeliness of the method. Orders to the broker are given the same day as the new data are obtained. When filled, a new order is given immediately which stops the open order and establishes a new position when filled. On November 8, for example, a buy was executed at 137.50 during trading hours, and an order to fill two at 133.70 was given following the market close.

Let's go through another example, this time in more detail. Assume it is November 15, that you have just consulted your broker, and he has given you high, low, and closing price data for the particular silver option you are following. Looking at the table, you will see that the last line, November 12, looks like this:

Date	High Price	Low Price	5-Day High	Waiting-Day High	5-Day Low	Waiting-Day Low
-	-	-	-	-	-	-
-	-	-	-	-	-	-
November 12	139.40	138.20	139.60	138.90	136.20	134.80

Entering the new data immediately, the next line now looks like this:

November 15   140.00 137.60

The next step is to look at the 5-day period November 9 through November 15 to determine the 5-day high and 5-day low. We see the day's high of 140.00 has become the new 5-day high, the 5-day low is 136.70 (November 10). Entering this data, the last line of the table now looks like this:

November 15   140.00 137.60 140.00 136.70

Now we have to determine the waiting-day high and low. We have been following an Extreme Price Channel with a 5-day channel and 3-day wait. Let us discover the waiting-day high and low from the data in columns 2 and 3. Since it is day 15, after the market close, we want November 16 to be the next day of our waiting

138

period; in this case, we want it to be day 3. This means that November 15 is day 2, and November 12 is day 1. Since November 12, 15, and 16 form our waiting period, this means that the five days before November 12 constitute our channel. Thus, November 5 through November 11 forms our 5-day channel. Looking at the prices in this period, we discover that the high was 139.60 and the low was 134.80; the high becomes our waiting-day high and the low our waiting-day low.

Looking at November 15 in the 5-day high column, we count back three days, using November 15 as the first day, for our waiting-day high—139.60. Similarly, on November 15 in the 5-day low column, we count back three days for the waiting-day low of 134.80. These two numbers which are the channel boundaries are entered in the proper columns. This completes the calculations for November 15. We now have the basis for the instructions to the broker.

There is an exception to the general rule just followed. Whenever there is an execution, the 5-day channel is updated immediately to *include* the most recent high and low prices. Thus, notice that on every execution date in Table 11-2 (November 8, November 22, November 29, December 27, January 4, and January 25), the waiting-day high is the same as the 5-day high, and the waiting-day low is the same as the 5-day low. This means that the 5-day high and low in columns 4 and 6 and the 5-day channel high and low (columns 5 and 7) have for this one day coincided. On the next day, the 5-day high (and low) begin to move away from the 5-day channel, a day at a time. The trader must be cautious. On the day following the execution, the trader will count back only two days for the waiting-day high or waiting-day low. On the second day after the execution, the trader again counts back three days, and continues doing so until another execution occurs. Note well, however, that if the trader is using other than a 3-day waiting period, the general rule is that to obtain a waiting day high or low (using a Table 11-2 for example), the trader will count back "n + 1" days, on the "nth" day after an execution.

The foregoing explanation may seem confusing. But actually the calculations are quite simple, once you've performed them a few times. "Dry run" it with data from the newspaper, or with the results in Table 11-2, giving the daily high and lows in columns 2 and 3.

Once the channel boundaries have been determined, then give your order to the broker. If the trader has a short position, then the relevant boundary is the upper one. If he has a long position, he is interested in the lower boundary. Referring to Table 11-2, suppose that it is November 16, and the trader has just calculated the channel boundaries. Since he is long a contract ahead, the trader is interested in liquidating and going short on the next penetration of the low boundary. On November 16, the new low boundary is calculated at 136.20, replacing the old low of 134.80. So after the market closes, the trader orders his broker to "Sell two July silver, New York, at 136.10 stop, cancel former order to sell two at 134.70." Selling two contracts has the effect of liquidating the long position and establishing a short position.

When a trader is short a contract, he is interested in the next penetration of the upper boundary and then concentrates on the waiting-day high. Referring to Table 11-2, on January 3 the trader orders the broker to "buy two July silver, New York, at 145.80, stop, cancel former order to buy two at 146.60 stop." Notice that the order to the broker is always a tick—10 points—above the waiting-day high and a tick below the waiting-day low. This is the signal that a breakout from the channel has occurred.

From reading Chapter 6 about the Closing Price Channel Method, it should be remembered that sometimes the closing price of the most recent day will be below an updated waiting-day low, or above an updated waiting-day high, because of the nature of the method. In these rare instances, a "market order" must be given instead of a specified price order. If the updated low boundary is 160.40, for example, but today's close is 159.80, our ordinary "sell two at 160.30 stop" is no good; we must order the broker to "sell two at the market." For this reason it is always necessary to compare the order with the closing price to be sure that a "buy stop" order is placed above the closing price, and a "sell stop" below it. An additional column to Table 11-2 could list each day's closing price.

MONITORING THE PRICE CHANNEL METHOD

Contrasted to the Extreme Price Channel Method, monitoring the Closing Price Channel Method is almost trivial. The signal in this method occurs when a closing price penetrates a channel boundary. The waiting period is only one day, meaning that the channel

140

TABLE 11-3

December 1972 Silver, New York

5-Day Closing Price Channel

Date 1971	Closing Price	Instruction to Broker Execute At		Execution
Sept. 1	166.00			
2	166.10			
3	164.80			
7	156.50			
8	155.30	Buy 2	166.20	
9	155.00	Buy 2	166.20	
10	153.00	Buy 2	164.90	
13	152.30	Buy 2	156.60	
14	154.60	Buy 2	155.40	
15	154.90	Sell 2	152.20	155.80B
16	156.20	Sell 2	152.20	
17	156.30	Sell 2	152.20	
20	157.60	Sell 2	154.50	
21	155.60	Sell 2	154.80	
22	155.60	Sell 2	155.50	
23	156.00	Buy 2	157.70	155.20S
24	155.80	Buy 2	157.70	
27	154.00	Buy 2	156.10	
28	154.60	Buy 2	156.10	
29	153.80	Buy 2	156.10	
30	153.50	Buy 2	155.90	
Oct. 1	153.20	Buy 2	154.70	
4	148.20	Buy 2	154.70	
5	146.30	Buy 2	153.90	
6	147.60	Buy 2	153.60	
7	148.30	Buy 2	153.30	
8	144.50	Buy 2	148.40	
12	142.50	Buy 2	148.40	
13	143.60	Buy 2	148.40	
14	143.80	Buy 2	148.40	
15	145.30	Buy 2	145.40	
18	146.70	Sell 2	142.40	146.10B

boundary is updated each day. In practice, then, monitoring the Closing Price Channel Method means simply looking at closing prices in an n-day and determining the boundaries by simply inspecting the method. Table 11-3 shows how to monitor a 5-day method using, for example, the December 1972 silver contract from September 1 through October 18. Here we shall assume that as of September 8, we are short one contract. At the close of the market on that day we inspect the five most recent closing prices, including the close on September 8. Since we are short one contract, we are interested in the upper channel boundary for our signal to reverse our position. This means that we are interested in the highest closing price in the series of five prices. This turns out to be 166.10, the closing price on September 2. Our order to the broker is to buy two contracts when the price penetrates this boundary—at 166.20. Updating the channel reveals no change. On September 10, the high closing price is 164.80, so our new order is to buy two at 164.90, canceling the old order. On September 14 our order is to buy two at 155.40, which is filled during the next day's market at 155.80. Immediately we inspect the series of closing prices for the low boundary (152.30) and instruct the broker to *sell* two at 152.20. The procedure is repeated each day, always updating the series of closing prices, and changing the order to the broker nearly every day.

12

Trading Procedure:
Instructing the Broker

None of the methods of trading discussed so far requires a complex order to buy or sell silver contracts.

For the Moving Average Method, a "market order" is given to the broker after the market has closed for the day and before it opens the next morning. Example: "Buy two December silver, New York market." Using this order the trader should get a fill (an execution) at or close to the opening price of the day. It is not necessary to specify the contract year if the option month that the speculator wants to trade is the near month. If there are two December options and the speculator wishes to trade the distant option, the year must be specified. The New York market must be specified, unless the trader wishes Board of Trade silver, in which case the designation Chicago is used.

For the Extreme Price Channel Method, a "buy stop" order or a "sell stop" order is given to the broker. Examples: "Buy two December silver, 156.30, stop" or "Sell two December silver, 150.40, stop." A "buy stop" order is only given at a price which is above the current market price. A "sell stop" is only given at a price which is below the market price. Once in a while, when trading the Extreme Price Channel Method, it will not be possible to give a buy or sell stop order because the market price closed above (for buy orders) or below (for sell orders) the price which would otherwise be given the broker. In this case, a "market" order is specified and given the same way as for the Moving Average Cross-over Method.

For the Closing Price Channel Method, a buy or sell stop order is given to the broker, the same as with the Extreme Price Channel Method. Examples: "Buy two March 73 silver, 193.20, stop" and "Sell two March silver, 210.50 stop." The difficulty sometimes experienced with the Extreme Price Channel Method is not shared by the Closing Price Channel Method; therefore no "market" orders are ever used in trading the Closing Price Channel Method.

In practice, the above instructions are too abbreviated for clarity's sake. The order must specify how many contracts are new longs or shorts, and how many are offsetting positions. Additionally, open orders must be canceled—if they are not, unintended transactions will occur, often to the surprise of the trader. Thus, a complete market would be given this way: "Buy two December silver, New York Market; one new, one offset"

Some complete stop orders are given this way: "Buy two March Silver, 193.20, stop, GTC, One new, one offset; CFO buy two at 195.80," and "sell two March silver, 210.50, stop, GTC, one new, one offset; CFO sell two at 206.90." GTC means "good till canceled." This informs the broker that the order is to remain open until filled or canceled. CFO is "cancel former order." The CFO order is an integral part in trading with the price channel methods, so close attention must be given to cancellation or the trader might discover he has unintentionally bought or sold contracts. Forgetting to cancel former orders usually turns out to be quite costly.

A format has been given (see Tables 12-1, 13-1, 13-2, and 13-3) in which instructions to the broker are recorded systematically along with the calculations that shape the order. If several methods are used, it can become confusing and cumbersome to have the orders to the broker on several sheets of paper. We suggest a summary sheet so that it can be read quickly. A summary sheet facilitates double-checking orders to the broker and lets the trader compare the open orders showing with the those open orders on the broker's records. When trading heavily, this comparison should be made at least once a week to eliminate as much paper-work error as possible. One way to keep such a summary sheet is a simple chronological listing as in Table 12-1.

TABLE 12-1

Orders to Broker

Summary Sheet

	Date	Buy/Sell	Option	Commodity	Price	Type of Order		New Off-set		Cancel Former Order	
E	1/3/72	Buy 2	July 72	Silver	145.80	Stop	GTC	1	1	Buy 2	146.60
X	1/4/72	Sell 2	July 72	Silver	139.90	Stop	GTC	1	1	—	—
E	1/5/72	Sell 2	Dec. 72	Silver	Market	—	—	1	1	—	—
E	1/7/72	Buy 2	Dec. 72	Silver	Market	—	—	1	1	—	—
X	1/7/72	Sell 2	July 72	Silver	140.90	Stop	GTC	1	1	Sell 2	139.90
X	1/10/72	Sell 2	July 72	Silver	141.50	Stop	GTC	1	1	Sell 2	140.90
X	1/11/72	Sell 2	July 72	Silver	142.10	Stop	GTC	1	1	Sell 2	141.50
X	1/12/72	Sell 2	July 72	Silver	144.30	Stop	GTC	1	1	Sell 2	142.10
X	1/13/72	Sell 2	July 72	Silver	145.90	Stop	GTC	1	1	Sell 2	144.30
X	1/14/72	Sell 2	July 72	Silver	146.30	Stop	GTC	1	1	Sell 2	145.90

13

Trading Procedure: Financial Position

There are probably people who can buy two or three silver contracts and then check with their broker weekly. Some of these people probably patronize gambling casinos and race tracks and approach the futures market as if it were a crap game or race and expect to make money on luck. Our book has not been written for them. We believe that commodities futures prices do not behave randomly and that purchase or sales of contracts can be a good investment if the market is approached sensibly.

A sensible attitude toward trading commodities includes the realization that methodological trading requires diligence. And one of the most important of details is the *financial position*.

Brokerage firms provide the trader with records of positions taken, records of gains and losses, and statements of account. But such records take time to prepare and often they are not up to date enough for the serious commodity trader.* Keeping on top of the situation requires maintaining daily records of your current financial position in the market. By doing this, you know, even sooner than your broker, how much excess margin you have in your account; or whether you are undermargined. By knowing the current financial position, the trader can use his funds optimally,

---

*A typical four-day delay from preparation to receipt is too long in the volatile futures market.

neither allowing sizable gains to lie fallow nor plunging into additional contracts when the margin to cover the transaction is insufficient.

There are many ways of keeping current records of the trader's position in the market. We suggest a method that's quick and comprehensive enough to insure that the trader knows where he stands at the close of the market each trading day—(1) a journal of open trades, (2) a summary of realized gains and losses, and (3) a journal of financial position.

An example of a journal of open trades is Table 13-1—a simple six-column schedule which is used to calculate the trader's net gain or loss at the end of each market day. The calculation is based on the closing price (see column 2). The first day has two entries— the first is the buy (or sell) price at which the fill occurred. At this price there is no point nor dollar change, and the cumulative net change shows only the commission which must be paid for this trade. The second entry on the first day is the closing price and the calculation which shows the net change in the trader's position (see Table 13-1 again). Subsequent entries and calculations are the same. Determine the difference between the closing prices and enter it as "point change" in column 3. Then multiply this change by the "point factor" in column 4 ($1 for one contract, $2 for two contracts, and so on), enter the product as the "dollar change" in column 5, and add this change to the previous balance in column 6, obtaining the "cumulative net change" in the position.

We have used all of the procedures developed and discussed in Chapters 11, 12, and 13 in our own trading. It is certainly possible to develop more sophisticated techniques. But our purpose has been to develop straightforward procedures which will generate the basic information needed for serious speculation without being so tedious that it takes the fun out of trading. There's nothing magical about our procedures, and you should feel free to experiment with whatever suits your purposes.

This is a "conservative" method of determining the equity in a particular trading position because of the round-turn commission which is deducted at the beginning of the series of journal entries. In practice, the commission is not taken by the brokerage house un-

TABLE 13-1

Contracts: One
Margin: $1000

September Silver
Trade No. 042

Date 1972	Closing Price	Point Change	Point Factor	Dollar Change	Cumulative Net Change
June 30	158.60B	—	1.00	—	(45.50)
30	158.00	−60	1.00	(60.00)	(105.50)
July 5	161.80	+380	1.00	380.00	274.50
6	169.80	+800	1.00	800.00	1074.50
7	171.30	+150	1.00	150.00	1224.50
10	170.50	−80	1.00	(80.00)	1144.50
11	170.70	+20	1.00	20.00	1164.50
12	176.30	+560	1.00	560.00	1724.50
13	174.90	−140	1.00	(140.00)	1584.50
14	176.30	+140	1.00	140.00	1724.50
17	179.10	+280	1.00	280.00	2004.50
18	178.00	−110	1.00	(110.00)	1894.50
19	178.30	+30	1.00	30.00	1924.50
20	177.10	−120	1.00	(120.00)	1804.50
21	176.30	−80	1.00	(80.00)	1724.50
24	177.40	+110	1.00	110.00	1834.50
25	179.10S	+170	1.00	170.00	2004.50

til the contract is liquidated. Therefore, an alternative method of keeping the journal of open trade would be to deduct the commission on the day in which the contract is liquidated, as shown in Table 13-2. This alternative method is easier for reconciling the trader's records with the monthly statement from the broker. Notice, however, that this method overstates the trader's equity on a closed-out basis by the amount of the commission (compare column 6 in Table 13-1 and 13-2). It should be mentioned, though, that the full amount of the trader's equity in the open position may be used in trading; insofar, then, as the trader is interested in maximizing use of his equity in further trading, the second method should be used because it reflects the full equity position. Insofar as the trader desires to proceed with financial caution, the first method is recommended because it reflects only the net amount that the trader will receive after closing the position.

TABLE 13-2

Contracts: One   September Silver
Margin: $1000   Trade No. 042

Date 1972	Closing Price	Point Change	Point Factor	Dollar Change	Cumulative Change
June 30	158.60B	—	1.00	—	—
30	158.00	−60	1.00	(60.00)	(60.00)
July 5	161.80	+380	1.00	380.00	320.00
6	169.80	+800	1.00	800.00	1120.00
7	171.30	+150	1.00	150.00	1270.00
10	170.50	−80	1.00	(80.00)	1190.00
11	170.70	+20	1.00	20.00	1210.00
12	176.30	+560	1.00	560.00	1770.00
13	174.90	−140	1.00	(140.00)	1630.00
14	176.30	+140	1.00	140.00	1770.00
17	179.10	+280	1.00	280.00	2050.00
18	178.00	−110	1.00	(110.00)	1940.00
19	178.30	+30	1.00	30.00	1970.00
20	177.10	−120	1.00	(120.00)	1850.00
21	176.30	−80	1.00	(80.00)	1770.00
24	177.40	+110	1.00	110.00	1880.00
25	179.10S	+170	1.00	170.00	2050.00
					(45.50)
					2004.50

Table 13-3 is an example of a summary of realized gains and losses. The purpose of this summary is to have an up-to-date record of the net gains (or losses) on closed-out positions. When the trade shown in the journal (Table 13-1) is closed out, it would be entered in the summary sheet as shown in the last line of Table 13-3.

Table 13-4 is an example of a journal of financial position. It is a nine-column schedule which shows each investment (including additions and withdrawals), realized gains and losses, equity in open trades, total margin available, effective and reserve margin, and percentage utilization of total margin. Columns 2 and 3 record the cash advanced to and received from the brokerage. Column 4 records the realized gains and losses on closed-out positions and is obtained directly from the summary sheet of realized gains and losses (see Table 13-3). Column 5 shows the equity in the open

150

TABLE 13-3

Summary of Realized Gains and Losses

Date Liquidated	Trade Number	Option Month	Commodity	Profit	Loss	Cumulative Total
Nov. 19	001	July 72	Silver		(115.50)	(115.50)
Dec. 22	002	July 72	Silver	474.50		359.00
Jan. 4	003	Sept. 72	Silver	14.50		373.50
5	004	July 72	Silver		(205.50)	168.00
24	005	July 72	Silver	604.50		772.50
31	006	July 72	Silver		(255.50)	517.00
Feb. 8	007	July 72	Silver	114.50		631.50
18	008	Sept. 72	Silver		(155.50)	476.00
22	009	Dec. 72	Silver		(185.50)	290.50
28	010	Dec. 72	Silver	224.50		515.00
Mar. 2	012	July 72	Silver	354.50		869.50
14	011	Dec. 72	Silver	554.50		1424.00
20	013	Dec. 72	Silver		(255.50)	1168.50
22	014	July 72	Silver		(325.50)	843.00
27	015	Dec. 72	Silver		(265.50)	577.50
April 11	016	Sept. 72	Silver	154.50		732.00
25	017	Sept. 72	Silver	464.50		1196.50
.	.	.	.	.	.	.
.	.	.	.	.	.	.
.	.	.	.	.	.	.
July 25	042	Sept. 72	Silver	2004.50		3780.00

trades at the end of each market day, and is obtained by adding up the cumulative total from each open trade position (column 6 in Table 13-1 and 13-2). The total margin available (column 6) is calculated by adding columns 3, 4, and 5. This is the maximum amount of money at the trader's disposal. This is also the amount which should agree with the statement of account received at the end of the month from the brokerage firm. Column 7 records the margin being used, the effective margin. In the example shown, the trader begins speculation with two contracts of silver; therefore, the effective margin is $2,000. Column 8 records the "unused" or reserve portion of the total margin available; this figure represents the "cushion" with which the trader expects to absorb a series of market losses, which is certain to come (see Chapter 14 on trading strategies). The reserve margin in column

151

TABLE 13-4

Financial Position

Date 1972	Additions or Withdrawals	Cash Investment	Realized Gains & Losses	Equity in Open Trades	Total Margin	Effective Margin	Reserve Margin	Percent Utilization	Liquidity Ratio
2/15	4000.00	4000.00	—	—	4000.00	—	4000.00	—	—
2/16		4000.00	—	(360.00)	3640.00	2000.00	1640.00	55%	1.82
2/17		4000.00	—	(170.00)	3830.00	2000.00	1830.00	52	1.92
2/18		4000.00	(155.50)	(30.00)	3814.50	2000.00	1814.50	52	1.91
2/22		4000.00	(341.00)	(110.00)	3549.00	2000.00	1549.00	56	1.77
2/23		4000.00	(341.00)	(190.00)	3469.00	2000.00	1469.00	58	1.73
2/24		4000.00	(341.00)	(130.00)	3529.00	2000.00	1529.00	57	1.76
2/25		4000.00	(341.00)	60.00	3719.00	2000.00	1719.00	54	1.86
2/28		4000.00	(116.50)	140.00	4023.50	2000.00	2023.50	50	2.01
2/29		4000.00	(116.50)	340.00	4223.50	2000.00	2223.50	47	2.11
.	.	.	.	.	.	.	.	.	.
3/1		4000.00	(116.50)	800.00	4683.50	2000.00	2683.50	43	2.34
3/2		4000.00	238.00	650.00	4888.00	2000.00	2888.00	41	2.44
3/3		4000.00	238.00	1070.00	5308.00	2000.00	3308.00	38	2.65
7/25		4000.00	3780.00	1160.00	8940.00	3000.00	5940.00	34	2.78
7/26	(1000.00)	3000.00	3780.00	820.00	7600.00	3000.00	4600.00	39	2.53
7/27		3000.00	3780.00	1580.00	8360.00	4000.00	4360.00	48	2.09
7/28	(1000.00)	2000.00	3780.00	1300.00	7080.00	4000.00	3080.00	56	1.77

8 is the difference between the total margin in column 6 and the effective margin in column 7. Column 9A records the percentage of effective margin which is being used. It is determined by dividing the effective margin by the total margin. The reciprocal of this number, that is, total margin divided by effective margin, is called the liquidity ratio, and shows at a glance the factor by which total margin exceeds effective margin. Both percent utilization and its reciprocal, "liquidity ratio," are important tools in trading and are discussed in Chapter 14. In practice only one of the two tools is needed for column 9; for our purposes we shall use the liquidity ratio, if only because it is usually easier to calculate. Referring to Table 13-4 it can be seen that the liquidity ratio can be changed abruptly and at will by additions or withdrawals of cash and/or by trading contracts.

14

Trading Strategies

AVOIDING GOING BROKE

You have just finished a chapter on selecting and monitoring the best of the Moving Average Cross-over, Extreme Price Channel, and Closing Price Channel methods. Now, let's deal with strategies. But, first, some legitimate questions must be aired. Should more than one method be used? If so, which? How much money should be kept in reserve? What profits as a percent of investment, including the reserve, should be expected? And, how much of profits should be reinvested?

We shall try to answer these questions as well as develop a trading strategy for a particular level of funding. Determination of the best allocation of funds requires a set of rules and a forecast of the strategy's results.

Any trading strategy faces the possibility of going broke. When the trading method at any time loses the entire investment, the speculator is, of course, wiped out. Since the original trading margin in silver futures traded on Commodity Exchange, Inc., is $1,000, the method can break the speculator whenever he gets behind as much as $1,000—that is, unless he maintains a *reserve*. If the speculator has no reserve in his trading account and the first trade loses even a dollar, the second trade cannot be made for he has $999 left. For a trading method to remain solvent, the speculator's account must at all times have at least $1,000 for margin, plus $45.50 for a round-turn commission.

A trading method requires a reserve, enabling the account to lose and still have at least $1,045.50. If $1,000,000 were deposited in the account, and only one contract were traded, for all practical purposes the speculator would be insured against being wiped out. Of course, the rate of return on the million-dollar investment would be abysmally low, unattractive, and pointless. So, a compromise must be struck. A speculator will choose a reserve that will minimize his chances of going broke, but not be so high that it minimizes the profit margin, plus the reserve.

In calculating the amount of reserve necessary for a single trading method, an acceptable degree of risk must be decided on. A good decision involves a risk of no greater than 1 percent. Such a strict policy is adopted because it allows for speculator's trepidations and errors. First of all, if a lower reserve is kept, several consecutive reversals, while not wiping out the speculator's account, will lose enough of the reserve to lower his account equity to below the $1,000 margin requirement. He would have to come up with more capital to continue trading. If the method during that time performed well, the speculator might feel defeated, and refrain from using any formal trading methods at all. Second, speculators make errors, so the reserve should be large enough to cover occasional slips. From time to time a speculator using a specific trading method will calculate the moving average or channel incorrectly, give a wrong order to the broker, or use the wrong option's process in calculating the channel or moving average. These errors almost invariably work against the speculator. However, sometimes an error will fortuitously cause an exit from a trade before the price moves contrary to the position in the market, or enter a trade and subsequently move the price in the direction of the position entered. From our experience, however, errors seem not to be at random or randomly distributed; usually they cause losses more often than profits. Yet, even if randomly distributed, the losses will be the size of the commissions, or $45.50 per trade. Thus, a reserve should be high enough to cover not only method-produced short-run losses, but error-produced net losses, plus commissions.

In this chapter the 1-percent-probability-of-going-broke level is

156

chosen.* The standard error of the mean was described in considerable detail in Chapter 10. Remember that about 68 percent of the means of repeated samples fall within one standard error (or deviation). There is, then, a 32-percent chance that a mean in a sample will fall outside the mean of the first sample; plus or minus the standard deviation. Sixteen percent of the samples will have means above the original mean plus the standard error, and 16 will be below.

One of our statistical assumptions concerning the sample of the 15 test options is that the relationship between the mean and the worst option loss is relatively constant. If the mean in another sample were $1,000 lower than in the sample tested, the worst option loss would also be $1,000. This would not be precise, but it's a sufficient guesstimate for our purposes.

Suppose there's a 16-percent chance that the mean of the 15-option sample is one standard error too high, and there's a 6.666-percent chance of doing as badly in one option as the greatest option loss. The chance of doing as poorly as the greatest option loss of one of the trading methods minus the standard error of its mean is 6.666 times 16 percent, or a 1-percent chance.

If the speculator keeps in reserve an amount sufficient to cover this great a loss, there will be *only* a 1-percent chance of going broke.

THE BEST METHOD, PLUS RESERVE

Now is the time to decide which trading method provides the greatest annual return on capital invested, including reserve. For an account sufficiently large to trade only one method, it is this method which would be used. Table 14-1 lists each method's in-

---

*It will not be appropriate here to explain in detail how to arrive at the level of reserve, given a 1-percent probability of going broke. This will be covered in Appendix C. The method used to determine the 1-percent level depends substantially on assumptions made regarding the sample's character.

In this chapter, it will be assumed that the actual distribution of the sample is representative of the method's behavior in the future. Thus, with this assumption, the greatest loss from a series of single-trade losses in an option will be taken as representative of how badly the option performs every one of 15 options. In other words, the greatest option loss in the test will be taken to be the level of loss with a 1/15- or 6 2/3-percent probability.

vested capital, annual return, and annual percent return. Not un-expectedly, Closing Price Channel Method 9 has the highest per-centage return, although its lead over the other methods, particu-larly 13, is smaller. Method 9 required a larger invested capital than 13, as both its greatest option loss and standard deviation are larger. The first two Closing Price Channel Methods are substan-tially superior to the 25- and 8-day Moving Average Method and the 21-day Closing Price Channel, primarily because the annual return of the last is smaller, and for the Moving Average Meth-od, because its invested capital requirement is much larger than the others. According to the table, the best trading strategy for a small account—which can trade only one method, including reserve—is the 9-day Closing Price Channel. With this method, a speculator with an account of about $2,400 can expect almost to double his money in a year.

Larger accounts, of course, produce larger problems. Trading ad-ditional contracts of the 9-day Closing Price Channel Trading Meth-od isn't the best strategy because when selecting the "right" com-bination of methods, the reserve requirements can be reduced.

Suppose two trading methods complemented each other com-pletely, in the sense that when one method had a losing option, the other always had a profit in that option, and that profit was always larger than the greatest option loss of the other method, plus the standard error of the other methods. In this case, no re-serve would be required at all, because the methods in conjunc-tion would produce a profit on each option. In this case, using the two together would yield higher returns on capital than trading two options of the best of the two methods. Elimination of the reserve requirement will more than compensate for the lower average return. Rarely do trading methods completely complement each other and it will not be possible to eliminate the reserve. But if two of the four methods partially complement each other, the re-serve requirement can be reduced. By inspecting Table 15-4 can be seen the extent to which the four acceptable methods tend to have losing options in tandem, and the extent to which they seem to win when the others lose. In fact, none of the four meth-ods under consideration loses during an option any other of the four loses, with the mean profit of each method exceeding the re-serve requirements of any other method.

TABLE 14-1

ANNUAL RETURN ON INVESTED CAPITAL

METHOD	INVESTED CAPITAL*	ANNUAL RETURN**	PERCENT
Closing Price Channel - 13	$2102	$2149	91
Closing Price Channel - 9	$2386	$2628	98
Moving Average 25.8	$2557	$1934	67
Closing Price Channel - 21	$2156	$1653	68

*Invested capital calculated as margin requirement ($1,000) added to reserve requirement.

**Annual return calculated as 75 percent of the option return, as an option of silver on Commodity Exchange trades approximately 16 months, excluding the spot month.

Yet, the sample of 15 options is not very large as statistical sampling goes. It would be difficult to have confidence in eliminating the reserve requirement. To do so would require a much larger sample, one that is not available, as silver has not been actively traded long enough. Without a larger sample, on what criteria should the reserve be reduced when trading two or more methods? One way is inspecting the kind of trading method as a whole against another kind, and using this as representative of the individual variations of that method. Thus, it can be seen that the two very bad options for moving averages, September and December 1968, were options in which no closing price channels lost money. Similarly, the worst option for closing price channels, December 1971, was an option in which every Moving Average Method was profitable. Conversely, the July 1969 option was one where both methods were treated about the same with some variations producing profits, and others producing losses.

The problem within a class of trading methods, say closing price channels, is more difficult. One could calculate the average correlation of losing options between every pair of variations, and take that as representative, but it simply is not accurate, as individual variations perform so differently. This criticism can also be leveled at the average of a method as representative of each variation when considering using both a Moving Average Method and a Closing Price Channel Method.

From doing distribution and correlation tests, it can be shown that closing price channels have no particular tendency to lose or profit together. The frequency of the number of options that win or lose in the various options are close to a random distribution, what one would expect if he generated the numbers by random, using a mean of one losing method per option. You can check this by jotting down how many options showed one, two, and three losses. There were 15 total losing options among all the Closing Price Channel methods. If there's little correlation, there will be more options with one losing method, the average, than any other number of losing methods, and fewer on each side, as the very popular bell-shaped curve (normal distribution).

Similarly, there's a negative correlation between moving average and closing price channels. When a closing price channel loses, you can be fairly confident that the moving average will not, and *vice versa*. The data clearly show this.

Because of the low frequency of losses among the 13- and 9- day Closing Price Channel Trading methods, there will be little likelihood that both will lose in the same option, although one winning enough to overcome the loss of the other is a complicated matter for calculation. Let it be concluded that the reserve requirement, when using any two or more methods together, can be reduced by about half with an actual increase in safety.

To trade two trading methods, one contract each, the 9-day Closing Price Channel Method should be used in conjunction with the 13-day one. The requirements are $2,000 for margin plus half of the combined reserve requirements. This is $1,244 in reserve, plus $2,000 margin, for a total of $3,244. The expected return would be the sum of the expected returns for each method, or $4,246. This produces about 131 percent profit per year—a very good investment. The profits of any other group of two or more of the four methods can be calculated in the same way.

15

Selecting the Best Methods

Thirteen profitable trading methods were presented in the last three chapters—five Moving Average methods, two Extreme Price Channel methods, and six Closing Price Channel methods. Unless a speculator were wealthy he could not trade all these methods, and even then such a trading strategy might not be optimal. Since the best of the 13 methods should be selected carefully, we shall discuss in this chapter what seem to be important criteria for the selection.

The most natural criteria are the profits generated by a trading method during an historical test. If one trading method produces substantially more profit than another, it would seem better to choose that method. From a previous chapter, we recognize the need to be confident in a trading method, and have selected the t-statistic as that measure of confidence. It would seem that to select the finest trading methods from those profitable methods presented, a list of the profitability and t-statistics of the methods should be assembled. Those falling short of a specified t-value should be eliminated, and those with the highest profits be selected as the best method.

Table 15-1 ranks the trading methods by their total profitability. The best produced $52,555 over 15 options, the worst $23,142. Their respective average profits per option occupies the last column.

161

It is first seen that the Extreme Price Channel Methods fall short of the Moving Cross-Over Average and Closing Price Channel Methods, and that the latter as a whole produce somewhat better results than Moving Averages as a whole.

TABLE 15-1

Trading Methods Ranked by Total Profit

Method	Variation	Total Profit Over 15 Options	Average Profit Per Option
CPC	9 day	52555	3503.7
MA	30 and 8 days	46230	3082.0
CPC	13 day	42977	2865.1
MA	25 and 8 days	38685	2579.0
CPC	17 day	35686	2379.1
CPC	21 day	33005	2204.3
MA	30 and 5 days	32700	2180.0
CPC	37 day	32335	2155.7
MA	40 and 5 days	32155	2143.7
MA	25 and 5 days	27990	1866.0
CPC	33 day	26705	1780.3
EPC	17 and 3 days	26160	1744.0
EPC	13 and 3 days	23142	1542.8

CPC = closing price channel
MA = moving average
EPC = extreme price channel

A selection method based only on total profitability and t-statistics is inadequate. It lacks consideration of two important criteria: first, the number of years a trading method lost money; secondly, the worst loss in any one year by a trading method. These two criteria can substantially affect a trading strategy—the first because considerations other than long-range profit must be accounted for; the second because a good trading strategy keeps enough money in reserve to cover bad losses. It does a speculator no good to expect a long-range high profit if he is wiped out in the short run. Ultimately, the expected profit of a trading method must be calculated not only on the money required for securing a contract of silver futures, but on the money required in reserve to cover the poor years that can be expected from time to time.

The proper approach of trading method selection will set minimum standards of performance in several criteria, and then choose the most profitable from the methods meeting the specifications. This, then, is our approach. The three criteria preceding profitability are the *t-statistic, the percent of options with profitable results,* and *the greatest loss in one option.*

T-Statistic. The t-statistic measures the probability the results of an experiment are due to chance. The greater the variability from year to year, the greater this probability. The higher the t-statistic, the lower this probability. As discussed in Chapter 10, the value of a t-statistic is translated into a probability that the results of the experiment are not a result of chance. The probability level is based on the number in the sample. As this test included 15 options of silver, its sample size is 15; the confidence level associated with the calculated t-statistic is for a sample of 15.

How confident should a speculator be that the results of his test are not due to chance? 50 percent? 90 percent? Or higher? The minimum criterion in this chapter is *99 percent.*

Table 15-2 ranks the trading methds by their t-statistic. Notice that the extreme price channels, lowest ranked by profits, are also lowest ranked by confidence. And, although lowest ranked, their confidence remains above 90 percent. In fact, only one method is lower than 95 percent confident. The 13-day Closing Price Channel Method has a far higher t-statistic than any other method. Second is the 9-day closing price channel. In fact, the closing price channels increase their superiority over any other method when comparing their relative levels of confidence.

A 99-percent confidence level is insisted upon because the market is not an unchanging process. The conditions under which the tests are performed are always changing. And, although the chances in the future are not unlike the conditions under which the market was tested in the past, they are not the same either. Nor do the various conditions common to both the past and future remain in the same proportions, or over similar periods of time. A number of conditions affect the behavior of speculators, and hence the behavior of prices.

TABLE 15-2

Trading Methods Ranked By T-Statistic

Method	Variation	T-Statistic	Confidence
CPC	13 day	6.484	99+
CPC	9 day	5.032	99+
MA	25 and 8 days	4.507	99+
CPC	21 day	4.448	99+
MA	30 and 8 days	4.010	99+
CPC	17 day	3.477	99+
CPC	37 day	3.289	99+
MA	40 and 5 days	3.239	99+
MA	25 and 5 days	2.812	98.5
MA	30 and 5 days	2.692	98
CPC	33 day	2.684	98
EPC	17 and 3 days	2.386	96.5
EPC	13 and 3 days	2.109	94.5

CPC = closing price channels
EPC = extreme price channels
MA = moving averages

The proportion of professional versus amateur speculators in the market affects the behavior of prices. Professional speculators are less apt to act on unfounded rumor, are more likely to act promptly, and likelier to discount conditions that affect the supply or demand for silver in advance. This, of course, alters the behavior of prices. Sometimes there are more, sometimes fewer, professionals, and the average ratio may change in the future, affecting the behavior of the market.

Competing investments may draw money from or into the market, depending on their current attractiveness. Gold, gold and silver coins, jewelry, and gold and silver mining stocks are all direct competitors of silver futures. Because they influence money entering or leaving speculation in silver, the market will behave differently. Although these investments have affected the market in the period over which the tests were made, and the trading methods proved profitable in these periods, they won't affect the market the same way in the future.

Indirectly competing investments also affect the behavior of speculators in silver futures. Bullish or bearish expectations of the stock market will cause money to enter or leave. Bond yields, return on real estate investment, and expectations for starting a new business will all affect the market in the future, as they have in the past.

Attitudes on silver *per se* as a speculative vehicle for investment will alter the behavior of the market. These attitudes are somewhat based on expectations of monetary stability and the likelihood of devaluation. However unlikely, the prospects of sensible monetary management by the governments of Western Europe, Japan, and the United States would decrease silver's attractiveness as a speculative vehicle. And, although this is unlikely, governments act more or less irresponsibly with money supplies. When they do act outrageously more people enter the silver market, causing greater autocorrelation in its movements, as new speculators tend to be less professional, and respond less rationally to rumor and the advice of financial services.

For these reasons, a speculator wants a *robust* method. It should perform consistently over an enormous number of market conditions, monetary instability, boom, recession, bullish and bearish stock markets, during times of large and small numbers of amateur speculators. As these conditions have all occurred during the period of testing, a method that performed consistently in these times is likely to perform that way in the future, even though the conditions in the market will always be changing.

Thus, the minimum criteria selected for the t-statistic is 99-percent proof. Referring again to Table 15-2, only five methods do not qualify. This is indicative of the strength of the trading methods. Those with t-statistics exceeding 4.0 have confidences that are significantly higher than 99 percent, close to 99.5 percent. After eliminating those with low t-statistics from the list of candidates, the remaining trading methods are:

Method	Variation
Closing Price Channel	13-day
Closing Price Channel	9-day
Moving Average	25- and 8-day
Closing Price Channel	21-day
Moving Average	30- and 8-day
Closing Price Channel	17-day
Closing Price Channel	37-day
Moving Average	40- and 5-day

Of the eight trading methods remaining as candidates for use, five are closing price channels, and three are moving averages.

Percent of Options with Profitable Results. A good minimum criteron here, although subjectively chosen, is four or five options profitable. A subjective consideration is necessary, because inclusion of this criterion at all is based on the psychology of a speculator. A trading method with too high a proportion of losing options will cause discouragement to a speculator. Persons have time preferences; they will usually choose a moderate amount of money now rather than somewhat more in the future. Small or moderate annual profits will put them far more at ease than methods with frequent losing years and fabulous profits during winning years. A trading method with good long-run results but with frequent losing options will probably not be used after a couple of losing years. The speculator will have doubts about it, will suffer from anxiety, and decide the long-run profits are not worth the ulcers resulting from the short-run poor performance. Security, like profits, is a goal of the speculator. It can easily be shown that maximum long-run profits are not the exclusive motivation of economic activity.

Suppose a very rich man, in fact an infinitely rich man, gave you the following proposition. You could have \$5,000 now, or receive 2^n dollars with the probability of 2^{-n}.

A number N would be picked with the probability 2^{-n}. 2 to the $-N$ power is $\frac{1}{2}^n$. The chance of getting \$1 is 50 percent. The chance of getting \$64 is $\frac{1}{64}$. It can be proved that the expected return, statistically, from this game is infinite. Therefore, if a person were concerned only with the maximization of profit without considerations of security or likelihood, he would choose the game over the

166

$5,000. But the chances of receiving as much as $5,000 in the game are one in 5,000. Almost everyone would choose the $5,000.

To a less extreme degree, this is what we face in speculation. To be secure, perhaps four of five years—or 80 percent of the options —should be profitable. Table 15-3 ranks the trading methods by percentage of profitable options. Only one method produced a profit every year, but nine of the thirteen qualified. All methods that qualified on the basis of the t-statistic qualified on the basis of number of profitable years. This is not surprising, as unprofitable years increase the variability of a sample, which lowers the sample t-statistic. Nevertheless, it certainly was possible, though unlikely, that a method with a sufficiently large t-statistic would have had fewer than 80 percent profitable options, so it was tested. So, the same eight candidates remain.

TABLE 15-3

Trading Methods Ranked By Percent Of Options Profitable

Method	Variation	Options	Profit-able	Precent
CPC	13 day	15	15	100
CPC	9 day	15	14	93.3
MA	40 and 5 day	15	13	86.7
MA	30 and 8 day	15	13	86.7
MA	25 and 8 day	15	13	86.7
MA	30 and 5 day	15	12	80
CPC	37 day	15	12	80
CPC	33 day	15	12	80
CPC	21 day	15	12	80
MA	25 and 5 day	15	11	73.3
EPC	13 and 3 day	15	11	73.3
CPC	17 day	15	11	73.3
EPC	17 and 3 day	15	10	66.7

Qualifiers 80 percent and above.
Nine of 13 trading methods qualify.
CPC = closing price channels
EPC = extreme price channels
MA = moving average

For convenience, Table 15-4 lists each option with losses for each trading method. Closing Price Channel Method 37, for example, was unprofitable in the July 1968, May 1970, and December 1971 options. Certain options, such as the December 1968 and July 1969 options, were unusually harsh on trading methods. Also, moving averages and closing price channels apparently complement each other, concentrating their losses in different options. This may prove useful in selecting two or more methods with which to speculate. Choosing methods that otherwise qualify by their complementary results in these charts can help smooth out losing years, while picking methods that tend to do well and poorly together may only magnify losing and winning years.

Greatest Loss in One Option. Suppose a speculator had a trading method that produced an average of $2,000 profit per year on a silver futures contract but could lose as much as $1,500 in one year. If the first year was that year, and the speculator only had enough money for one contract, he would be wiped out. The average profit of $2,000 per option would be of no value to him. To insure against being wiped out, he would need to keep at least $1,500 in reserve, and additionally put up $1,000 for trading.*

If the $1,500 kept in reserve is considered part of the actual investment, as well it should be considered, the $2,000 average option profit, that conceivably could have been looked upon as 200 percent, then becomes only 80 percent. Next suppose a trading method produced an average of $1,500 an option profit, $500 less than the first method, but lost only as much as $500 in a single option. The speculator using this method need keep only $500 in reserve. The $1,500 profit is made on a $1,500 investment ($1,000 margin requirement, plus $500 reserve). The profit is 100 percent.

Of the total money used for speculating, the less needed for reserve requirements releases more for purchase of additional contracts, thereby increasing the employment of and profit from the funds.

Reserve requirements are one reason for considering the greatest loss in one option of a trading method. The other, as with the percentage of profitable options, is psychological. A trading meth-

---

*Actually, he requires more than a $1,500 reserve, as this number is the greatest annual loss, while losses in a shorter period of time can be even higher.

TABLE 15-4

Options With Losses For Each Trading Method

Method	Jul 68	Jul 69	Jul 70	Jul 71	Dec 67	Dec 68	Dec 69	Dec 70	Dec 71	Sep 68	Sep 69	Sep 70	Sep 71	May 70	Jan 72
CPC 37	X								X					X	
CPC 33				X				X	X				X		
CPC 21		X													
CPC 17		X							X		X			X	X
CPC 13							X								
CPC 9													X		
EPC 17-3		X				X			X		X				
EPC 13-3		X					X				X			X	X
MA 40-5						X				X					
MA 30-8						X				X					
MA 30-5		X				X				X					
MA 25-8				X		X									
MA 25-5		X				X				X	X				

CPC = closing price channels
MA = moving averages
EPC = extreme price channels

169

od, no matter how profitable overall, will cause severe anxiety in a speculator if it loses too much in one option. He will, in fact, probably cease using it. A good trading method will not only produce profits, but prevent ulcers. From our trading, we know it is difficult to continue using methods that are subject to severe losses, no matter if only temporary.

There are formal statistical procedures for deciding the maximum acceptable loss in one option for a trading method, based on its profitability, but since we have avoided making this book into a statistical treatise, a less formal procedure will suffice.

The maximum acceptable loss in one option will be chosen to be the amount of the original margin, or $1,000. Those trading methods losing more than $1,000 in any one option will be rejected as requiring too much reserve, and increasing the speculator's anxiety.

Referring to Table 15-5, only four methods qualify—all of which qualified on previous grounds. Those methods previously qualified which are to be rejected here are the 30- and 8-day Moving Average Cross-over Method, the 17- and 37-day Closing Price Channel methods, and the 40- and 5-day Moving Averages. Not surprisingly, the four still qualifying were those with the highest t-statistics. This is another indication of how powerful formal statistical procedures really are. Many "experts" tend to belittle the use of statistical techniques in practical matters of speculation. But these techniques have proved their worth in sales assignments, transportation routing, inventory control, purchasing, and personnel assignment. Their results in the analysis of price behavior is just as rewarding. The t-statistic has chosen those methods that intuition and common-sense analysis also choose, and chooses them more accurately.

Four trading methods remain as suitable for trading (Table 15-6). They have passed strict qualifications, and a speculator can have a high degree of confidence in their robustness in the silver market.

TABLE 15-5

Trading Methods Ranked By Greatest Loss In One Option

Method	Variation	Loss	Option Occurred
CPC	13 day	None	
CPC	21 day	−660	72 Jan.
CPC	9 day	−690	71 Sept.
MA	25 and 8 day	−985	68 Dec.
CPC	37 day	−1125	71 Dec.
MA	30 and 8 day	−1170	68 Sept.
CPC	17 day	−1555	69 Dec.
CPC	33 day	−2055	71 July
MA	25 and 5 day	−2310	69 July
MA	40 and 5 day	−2375	68 Dec.
EPC	17 and 3 day	−3345	69 July
EPC	13 and 3 day	−3858	69 Sept.
MA	30 and 5 day	−3875	69 Dec.

CPC = closing price channel
MA = moving average
EPC = extreme price channel

TABLE 15-6
THE FOUR METHODS
MOST SUITABLE FOR TRADING

Method	Percent Profitable Options	T-Statistic	Total Profit	Greatest Loss
Closing Price Channel 13	1.000	6.484	42977	NONE
Closing Price Channel 9	.933	5.032	52555	-690
Moving Average 25-8	.867	4.507	38685	-985
Closing Price Channel 21	.800	4.448	33005	-660

Glossary of Commodity Market Terms

These terms are those most commonly employed in commodity market literature. Not all are of trading significance—some refer only to the cash market of exchange business. Nevertheless, it will be useful to be familiar with these terms in order to eliminate confusion and gain insights.

Accumulate: Heavy buying of a commodity futures contract by traders over a long time; indication of heavy demand at the price range in which the commodity is trading. Accumulation usually precedes an upward price movement.

Actuals: The physical supply of the commodity existing at any given time. The actual supply, as opposed to futures.

Afloats: Commodity supply on sea vessels ready for shipment to a destination, or en route to destination. Does not include commodity supply in port ready for unloading.

Arbitrage: Purchase and sale of identical quantities of a cash commodity or of the same months' futures contracts in different markets at the same time. This is done to profit from a difference in prices for the commodity now or for a future delivery that is believed to be temporary. The high price is sold and the low price bought in the belief the disparity between the two prices will diminish or disappear altogether.

At the Market: An order by a trader to a broker to buy or sell a futures contract at the market price at the time the order is received.

Backwardation: A situation in the futures market of a commodity where the price of the commodity in near months exceeds the price of the commodity in distant months.

Basis: The price difference over or under a designated future at which a commodity is sold or quoted.

Basis Grade: The standard grade, or quality, of a commodity set by the exchange for any futures contract. Superior or inferior grades within specified limits may be substituted at premiums or discounts determined by the exchange.

Bear: A speculator expecting lower prices.

Bear Market: A commodity market, cash and futures, on which prices are declining steadily.

Bid: A price at which an offer to purchase a commodity is made; it is subject to immediate acceptance or else becomes void.

Break: A large decline in prices in a short period of trading.

Broker: A representative of a member firm who takes orders from traders; a floor or "pit" representative of a member firm.

Bulge: A large rise in prices in a short period of trading.

Bull: A speculator expecting higher prices.

Bull Market: A commodity market, cash and futures, on which prices are rising steadily.

Buy on Close: To buy a contract at the end of a trading session.

Buy on Opening: To buy a contract at the beginning of a trading session.

C. & F.:   Cost and freight paid to a port of destination.

Carrying Charges: Warehouse storage charges, interest, insurance and other charges levied when storing a commodity over a period of time. When a commodity has several futures contracts in between harvests, the carrying charges will be manifested in higher prices in succeeding delivery futures months.

Cash Commodity: The actual physical commodity as distinguished from futures contracts. Called spot commodities.

CCC: Commodity Credit Corporation.

C.E.A.:   Commodity Exchange Authority.

Certified Stocks: Supplies of a commodity inspected and certified for delivery in fulfullment of a futures contract by the exchange in question.

174

C.I.F.: Cost, insurance, freight paid or included to the port of destination when quoting the price of the commodity.

Clearances: The total marine shipments of a particular commodity on a specified date.

Clearing House: An agency of a commodity exchange which executes floor trading transactions by matching purchases and sales. The clearing house is also responsible for the financial behavior of its members and their conduct within the rules of the exchange.

Close: The time period at the end of the trading day during which all transactions are considered at the close.

Closing Price: The specific prices or price range at which sales at the close were transacted.

Commission: A fee charged by the exchange to members and by members to nonmembers for buying and selling a futures contract. The commission is always higher for nonmembers than for members.

Commission House: A business firm that executes trades in the name of its customers for the commission charged nonmembers.

Contract Grades: The definition by an exchange of which grades of a commodity are eligible for delivery on a cash or futures transaction, and at what premium or discount.

Cover: The liquidation of a short futures sale by buying an equal number of contracts in the same futures month.

Crop Year: The time period from one crop's harvest to its next. In soybeans this is September 1-August 31; for cotton August 1-July 31.

Day Orders: Orders to buy or sell a commodity that expire at the end of the trading day if not executed.

Deliverable Grades: See Contract Grades

Deliverable Stocks: See Certified Stocks.

Delivery: The tender and receipt of the specified amount of the commodity of deliverable grade in fulfillment of a futures contract; may also be tender and receipt of a warehouse receipt for the commodity.

Delivery Month: The named month during which a futures contract is subject to fulfillment.

Delivery Notice: A notice of a clearing member's intention to

175

deliver a stated quantity of commodity in settlement of a futures contract.

Delivery Points: Locations designated by commodity futures exchanges at which a commodity may be delivered in settlement of a futures contract.

Differentials: Premiums or discounts corresponding to superior and inferior quality of a commodity from a basic grade.

Discretionary Account: An account in which the trader agrees to permit orders to be placed by someone else without prior consultation.

Evening Up: A process by which a futures trader reduces his risk by liquidation or straddles.

Ex Pit Transactions: Trades executed elsewhere than the regular exchange pit.

F.A.Q.: Fair average quality.

Farm Prices: The prices received by farmers for their commodities, as published by the U.S. Department of Agriculture on the 15th of each month.

First Day Notice: The first day authorized by the exchange to issue notices of intention to deliver an actual commodity in settlement of a futures contract.

F.O.B.: Free on Board. Covers the cost of putting commodities on board but does not include delivery charges.

Forward Shipment: A contract for shipment of actual commodities in the future.

Futures: A contract on a commodity exchange to ship or deliver a commodity during a specific month in the future according to all the rules of the exchange regarding financing, quality, and quantity.

Grades: Different qualities of a commodity as defined by the exchange.

Grading Certificates: A formal paper issued by agents of the exchange certifying the quality of the commodity.

G.U.C.: Good until canceled. Refers to orders to buy or sell valid until canceled by the trader.

Hedge: The sale of futures contracts in a quantity offset by purchase of the commodity or ownership of the commodity; purchase of futures contracts offset by sales of the same commodity. Hedges are used by processors of a commodity to reduce the risk of loss through price fluctuation.

Inverted Market: See Backwardation.

Invisible Supply: The supply of a commodity held by wholesalers, producers, consumers and manufacturers which cannot be counted in official reports.

Job Lot: A quantity of cash or futures smaller than the normal contract. Used mostly in grains and cotton.

Last Trading Day: The last day an exchange permits trading a commodity in a particular futures month. Contracts not liquidated by the last trading day must be settled through actual delivery of the commodity.

Life of Contract: The period between the first trading day and the last trading day on any futures contract.

Limited Order: An order given by a trader requiring the broker only to buy or sell if certain restrictions are met; usually on price.

Liquidation: Any transaction offsetting a position in the market; if purchases have been made in a future, liquidating the position is selling the same month.

Loan Prices: The prices at which producers of a commodity obtain loans from the government for their product.

Long: A position of unhedged owning of a physical commodity or purchasing a commodity for future delivery.

Lot: A specified quantity of a commodity at a certain grade.

Margin: Cash posted as a guarantee to fulfill a futures contract; this is not partial payment for the commodity.

Margin Call: A demand to the trader for additional margin cash because of adverse price movements in the market.

Market Order: An order to buy or sell at the market price.

Negotiable Warehouse Receipt: A document issued by a warehouse guaranteeing the existence of, and sometimes the grade of a specified amount of the commodity.

Net Position: The difference between the open contracts purchased in a futures month of a commodity and the open contracts sold in the same month. We say a trader is three May potatoes net long.

Nominal Price: Price quotations on a future during a trading period on which no actual trading occurred.

177

Offer: The opposite of bid. A desire to sell at a certain price, canceled immediately if not executed.

On Opening: Execution of an order during the beginning of a trading day.

Open Contracts: Contracts bought or sold which have not been offset.

Open Interest: The number of open contracts in any given future or the total of futures months for a commodity. Never designates the combined total of open purchases and open sales, since both are required for one open contract.

Opening, The: The time period at the beginning of a trading session at which all transactions are designated "at the opening."

Opening Price: The price or price range at which trades are executed "at the opening."

Pit: A location on the exchange floor at which trading in a certain commodity is executed.

Point: The minimum unit price fluctuations on futures trading may be expressed.

Position: An open purchase or sale in a commodity or future.

Premium: The amount over which a unit of superior grade commodity brings compared to a unit of standard grade commodity (Basic grade).

Price Limit: The maximum fluctuation in price from the last day's close that the price of a commodity may make in today's trading session.

Range: The difference between the high price at which a commodity future is traded in one trading session, and the low price it is traded in one trading session.

Reaction: Either a price advance after a sharp decline; or a price decline after a sharp advance.

Ring: Like a pit, a circular platform on which trading is executed in a particular commodity and its futures.

Round Lot: See Lot.

Round Turn: A complete trading transaction including the initiation and liquidation of a trade.

Short: A position of unhedged selling of a physical commodity or selling short a commodity for future delivery.

Spot Commodity: See Actuals and Cash Commodity.

Spot Price: The price of a cash commodity at a specific time during a trading session.

Stop-Loss Order: An order to buy or sell only when the market reaches a specified price.

Straddle: Purchase of a commodity in one market and sale in another market, or purchase of one future month and sale in another future month.

Volume of Trading: The sum of futures transactions in a particular month or all the months of one commodity.

Appendix

SIMULTANEOUS TRADING

September 1972 Silver Contract—4 Method Trading

Date 1971	CPC-9 Long	CPC-9 Short	CPC-13 Long	CPC-13 Short	CPC-21 Long	CPC-21 Short	25 x 8 Long	25 x 8 Short	TOTAL Long	TOTAL Short	NET Long	NET Short
4/30	0	0	0	0	0	0	0	0	0	0	0	0
5/3	0	0	0	0	0	0	0	0	0	0	0	0
5/4	0	0	0	0	0	0	0	0	0	0	0	0
5/5	0	0	0	0	0	0	0	0	0	0	0	0
5/6	0	0	0	0	0	0	0	0	0	0	0	0
5/7	0	0	0	0	0	0	0	0	0	0	0	0
5/10	0	0	0	0	0	0	0	0	0	0	0	0
5/11	0	0	0	0	0	0	0	0	0	0	0	0
5/12	0	0	0	0	0	0	0	0	0	0	0	0
5/13	1	0	0	0	0	0	0	0	1	0	1	0
5/14	1	0	0	0	0	0	0	0	1	0	1	0
5/17	1	0	0	0	0	0	0	0	1	0	1	0
5/18	1	0	0	0	0	0	0	0	1	0	1	0
5/19	1	0	0	0	0	0	0	0	1	0	1	0
5/20	0	1	0	0	0	0	0	0	0	1	0	1
5/21	0	1	0	1	0	0	0	0	0	2	0	2

Date 1971	CPC-9 Long	CPC-9 Short	CPC-13 Long	CPC-13 Short	CPC-21 Long	CPC-21 Short	25 x 8 Long	25 x 8 Short	TOTAL Long	TOTAL Short	NET Long	NET Short
5/24	0	1	0	1	0	0	0	0	0	2	0	2
5/25	0	1	0	1	0	0	0	0	0	2	0	2
5/26	0	1	0	1	0	0	0	0	0	2	0	2
5/27	0	1	0	1	0	0	0	0	0	2	0	2
5/28	0	1	0	1	0	0	0	0	0	2	0	2
6/1	0	1	0	1	0	0	0	0	0	2	0	2
6/2	0	1	0	1	0	1	0	0	0	3	0	3
6/3	0	1	0	1	0	1	0	0	0	3	0	3
6/4	0	1	0	1	0	1	0	0	0	3	0	3
6/7	0	1	0	1	0	1	0	0	0	3	0	3
6/8	0	1	0	1	0	1	0	0	0	3	0	3
6/9	0	1	0	1	0	1	0	0	0	3	0	3
6/10	0	1	0	1	0	1	0	0	0	3	0	3
6/11	1	0	0	1	0	1	0	0	1	2	0	1
6/14	1	0	0	1	0	1	0	0	1	2	0	1
6/15	1	0	0	1	0	1	0	0	1	2	0	1
6/16	1	0	1	0	0	1	0	0	2	1	1	0
6/17	1	0	1	0	0	1	0	0	2	1	1	0
6/18	1	0	1	0	0	1	0	0	2	1	1	0
6/21	0	1	0	1	0	1	0	0	0	3	0	3
6/22	0	1	0	1	0	1	0	0	0	3	0	3
6/23	0	1	0	1	0	1	0	0	0	3	0	3
6/24	0	1	0	1	0	1	0	0	0	3	0	3
6/25	0	1	0	1	0	1	0	0	0	3	0	3
6/28	0	1	0	1	0	1	0	0	0	3	0	3
6/29	0	1	0	1	0	1	0	0	0	3	0	3
6/30	0	1	0	1	0	1	0	0	0	3	0	3
7/1	0	1	0	1	0	1	0	0	0	3	0	3
7/2	0	1	0	1	0	1	0	0	0	3	0	3
7/6	0	1	0	1	0	1	0	0	0	3	0	3
7/7	0	1	0	1	0	1	0	0	0	3	0	3
7/8	0	1	0	1	0	1	0	0	0	3	0	3
7/9	0	1	0	1	0	1	0	0	0	3	0	3
7/12	0	1	0	1	0	1	0	0	0	3	0	3
7/13	0	1	0	1	0	1	0	0	0	3	0	3
7/14	0	1	0	1	0	1	0	0	0	3	0	3

182

Date 1971	CPC-9 Long	CPC-9 Short	CPC-13 Long	CPC-13 Short	CPC-21 Long	CPC-21 Short	25 x 8 Long	25 x 8 Short	TOTAL Long	TOTAL Short	NET Long	NET Short
7/15	0	1	0	1	0	1	0	0	0	3	0	3
7/16	0	1	0	1	0	1	0	0	0	3	0	3
7/19	0	1	0	1	0	1	0	0	0	3	0	3
7/20	0	1	0	1	0	1	0	0	0	3	0	3
7/21	0	1	0	1	0	1	0	0	0	3	0	3
7/22	0	1	0	1	0	1	0	0	0	3	0	3
7/23	0	1	0	1	0	1	0	0	0	3	0	3
7/26	0	1	0	1	0	1	0	0	0	3	0	3
7/27	0	1	0	1	0	1	0	0	0	3	0	3
7/28	1	0	0	1	0	1	0	0	1	2	0	1
7/29	1	0	1	0	0	1	0	0	2	1	1	0
7/30	1	0	1	0	0	1	0	0	2	1	1	0
8/2	1	0	1	0	0	1	0	0	2	1	1	0
8/3	1	0	1	0	0	1	0	0	2	1	1	0
8/4	1	0	1	0	1	0	0	0	3	0	3	0
8/5	1	0	1	0	1	0	1	0	4	0	4	0
8/6	1	0	1	0	1	0	1	0	4	0	4	0
8/9	1	0	1	0	1	0	1	0	4	0	4	0
8/10	1	0	1	0	1	0	1	0	4	0	4	0
8/11	0	1	1	0	1	0	1	0	3	1	2	0
8/12	0	1	1	0	1	0	1	0	3	1	2	0
8/13	0	1	1	0	1	0	1	0	3	1	2	0
8/19	0	1	0	1	1	0	1	0	2	2	0	0
8/20	0	1	0	1	1	0	1	0	2	2	0	0
8/23	0	1	0	1	1	0	1	0	2	2	0	0
8/24	0	1	0	1	0	1	1	0	1	3	0	2
8/25	0	1	0	1	0	1	0	1	0	4	0	4
8/26	0	1	0	1	0	1	0	1	0	4	0	4
8/27	0	1	0	1	0	1	0	1	0	4	0	4
8/30	0	1	0	1	0	1	0	1	0	4	0	4
8/31	0	1	0	1	0	1	0	1	0	4	0	4
9/1	0	1	0	1	0	1	0	1	0	4	0	4
9/2	0	1	0	1	0	1	0	1	0	4	0	4
9/3	0	1	0	1	0	1	0	1	0	4	0	4
9/7	0	1	0	1	0	1	0	1	0	4	0	4
9/8	0	1	0	1	0	1	0	1	0	4	0	4

Date 1971	CPC-9 Long	CPC-9 Short	CPC-13 Long	CPC-13 Short	CPC-21 Long	CPC-21 Short	25 x 8 Long	25 x 8 Short	TOTAL Long	TOTAL Short	NET Long	NET Short
9/9	0	1	0	1	0	1	0	1	0	4	0	4
9/10	0	1	0	1	0	1	0	1	0	4	0	4
9/13	0	1	0	1	0	1	0	1	0	4	0	4
9/14	0	1	0	1	0	1	0	1	0	4	0	4
9/15	0	1	0	1	0	1	0	1	0	4	0	4
9/16	0	1	0	1	0	1	0	1	0	4	0	4
9/17	0	1	0	1	0	1	0	1	0	4	0	4
9/20	1	0	0	1	0	1	0	1	1	3	0	2
9/21	1	0	0	1	0	1	0	1	1	3	0	2
9/22	1	0	0	1	0	1	0	1	1	3	0	2
9/23	1	0	0	1	0	1	0	1	1	3	0	2
9/24	1	0	0	1	0	1	0	1	1	3	0	2
9/27	0	1	0	1	0	1	0	1	0	4	0	4
9/28	0	1	0	1	0	1	0	1	0	4	0	4
9/29	0	1	0	1	0	1	0	1	0	4	0	4
9/30	0	1	0	1	0	1	0	1	0	4	0	4
10/1	0	1	0	1	0	1	0	1	0	4	0	4
10/4	0	1	0	1	0	1	0	1	0	4	0	4
10/5	0	1	0	1	0	1	0	1	0	4	0	4
10/6	0	1	0	1	0	1	0	1	0	4	0	4
10/7	0	1	0	1	0	1	0	1	0	4	0	4
10/8	0	1	0	1	0	1	0	1	0	4	0	4
10/12	0	1	0	1	0	1	0	1	0	4	0	4
10/13	0	1	0	1	0	1	0	1	0	4	0	4
10/14	0	1	0	1	0	1	0	1	0	4	0	4
10/15	0	1	0	1	0	1	0	1	0	4	0	4
10/18	0	1	0	1	0	1	0	1	0	4	0	4
10/19	0	1	0	1	0	1	0	1	0	4	0	4
10/20	0	1	0	1	0	1	0	1	0	4	0	4
10/21	0	1	0	1	0	1	0	1	0	4	0	4
10/22	0	1	0	1	0	1	0	1	0	4	0	4
10/26	0	1	0	1	0	1	0	1	0	4	0	4
10/27	0	1	0	1	0	1	0	1	0	4	0	4
10/28	0	1	0	1	0	1	0	1	0	4	0	4
10/29	0	1	0	1	0	1	0	1	0	4	0	4
11/1	0	1	0	1	0	1	0	1	0	4	0	4

Date 1971	CPC-9 Long	CPC-9 Short	CPC-13 Long	CPC-13 Short	CPC-21 Long	CPC-21 Short	25 x 8 Long	25 x 8 Short	TOTAL Long	TOTAL Short	NET Long	NET Short
11/3	0	1	0	1	0	1	0	1	0	4	0	4
11/4	0	1	0	1	0	1	0	1	0	4	0	4
11/5	0	1	0	1	0	1	0	1	0	4	0	4
11/8	0	1	0	1	0	1	0	1	0	4	0	4
11/9	0	1	0	1	0	1	0	1	0	4	0	4
11/10	0	1	0	1	0	1	0	1	0	4	0	4
11/11	1	0	0	1	0	1	0	1	1	3	0	2
11/12	1	0	0	1	0	1	0	1	1	3	0	2
11/15	1	0	0	1	0	1	0	1	1	3	0	2
11/16	1	0	1	0	0	1	0	1	2	2	0	0
11/17	1	0	1	0	0	1	1	0	3	1	2	0
11/18	1	0	1	0	0	1	1	0	3	1	2	0
11/19	1	0	1	0	0	1	1	0	3	1	2	0
11/22	0	1	1	0	0	1	1	0	2	2	0	0
11/23	0	1	1	0	0	1	1	0	2	2	0	0
11/24	0	1	1	0	0	1	1	0	2	2	0	0
11/26	0	1	1	0	0	1	1	0	2	2	0	0
11/29	1	0	1	0	1	0	1	0	4	0	4	0
11/30	1	0	1	0	1	0	1	0	4	0	4	0
12/1	1	0	1	0	1	0	1	0	4	0	4	0
12/2	1	0	1	0	1	0	1	0	4	0	4	0
12/3	1	0	1	0	1	0	1	0	4	0	4	0
12/6	1	0	1	0	1	0	1	0	4	0	4	0
12/7	1	0	1	0	1	0	1	0	4	0	4	0
12/8	1	0	1	0	1	0	1	0	4	0	4	0
12/9	1	0	1	0	1	0	1	0	4	0	4	0
12/10	1	0	1	0	1	0	1	0	4	0	4	0
12/13	1	0	1	0	1	0	1	0	4	0	4	0
12/14	1	0	1	0	1	0	1	0	4	0	4	0
12/15	1	0	1	0	1	0	1	0	4	0	4	0
12/16	1	0	1	0	1	0	1	0	4	0	4	0
12/17	1	0	1	0	1	0	1	0	4	0	4	0
12/20	1	0	1	0	1	0	1	0	4	0	4	0
12/21	0	1	1	0	1	0	1	0	3	1	2	0
12/22	0	1	1	0	1	0	1	0	3	1	2	0
12/23	0	1	1	0	1	0	1	0	3	1	2	0

185

Date 1971-72	CPC-9 Long	CPC-9 Short	CPC-13 Long	CPC-13 Short	CPC-21 Long	CPC-21 Short	25 x 8 Long	25 x 8 Short	TOTAL Long	TOTAL Short	NET Long	NET Short
12/27	0	1	0	1	1	0	1	0	2	2	0	0
12/28	0	1	0	1	1	0	1	0	2	2	0	0
12/29	0	1	0	1	1	0	1	0	2	2	0	0
12/30	0	1	0	1	1	0	1	0	2	2	0	0
1/3	0	1	0	1	1	0	0	1	1	3	0	2
1/4	1	0	0	1	1	0	0	1	2	2	0	0
1/5	1	0	0	1	1	0	0	1	2	2	0	0
1/6	1	0	1	0	1	0	0	1	3	1	2	0
1/7	1	0	1	0	1	0	0	1	3	1	2	0
1/10	1	0	1	0	1	0	0	1	3	1	2	0
1/11	1	0	1	0	1	0	1	0	4	0	4	0
1/12	1	0	1	0	1	0	1	0	4	0	4	0
1/13	1	0	1	0	1	0	1	0	4	0	4	0
1/14	1	0	1	0	1	0	1	0	4	0	4	0
1/17	1	0	1	0	1	0	1	0	4	0	4	0
1/18	1	0	1	0	1	0	1	0	4	0	4	0
1/19	1	0	1	0	1	0	1	0	4	0	4	0
1/20	1	0	1	0	1	0	1	0	4	0	4	0
1/21	1	0	1	0	1	0	1	0	4	0	4	0
1/24	1	0	1	0	1	0	1	0	4	0	4	0
1/25	0	1	1	0	1	0	1	0	3	1	2	0
1/26	0	1	0	1	1	0	1	0	2	2	0	0
1/27	0	1	0	1	1	0	1	0	2	2	0	0
1/28	1	0	1	0	1	0	1	0	4	0	4	0
1/31	1	0	1	0	1	0	1	0	4	0	4	0
2/1	1	0	1	0	1	0	1	0	4	0	4	0
2/2	1	0	1	0	1	0	1	0	4	0	4	0
2/3	1	0	1	0	1	0	1	0	4	0	4	0
2/4	1	0	1	0	1	0	1	0	4	0	4	0
2/7	1	0	1	0	1	0	1	0	4	0	4	0
2/8	1	0	1	0	1	0	1	0	4	0	4	0
2/9	1	0	1	0	1	0	1	0	4	0	4	0
2/10	1	0	1	0	1	0	1	0	4	0	4	0
2/11	0	1	1	0	1	0	1	0	3	1	2	0
2/14	0	1	1	0	1	0	1	0	3	1	2	0
2/15	0	1	0	1	1	0	1	0	2	2	0	0

Date 1972	CPC-9 Long	Short	CPC-13 Long	Short	CPC-21 Long	Short	25 x 8 Long	Short	TOTAL Long	Short	NET Long	Short
2/16	0	1	0	1	0	1	1	0	1	3	0	2
2/17	0	1	0	1	0	1	0	1	0	4	0	4
2/18	0	1	0	1	0	1	0	1	0	4	0	4
2/22	0	1	0	1	0	1	0	1	0	4	0	4
2/23	0	1	0	1	0	1	0	1	0	4	0	4
2/24	0	1	0	1	0	1	0	1	0	4	0	4
2/25	0	1	0	1	0	1	0	1	0	4	0	4
2/28	0	1	0	1	0	1	0	1	0	4	0	4
2/29	0	1	0	1	0	1	0	1	0	4	0	4
3/1	0	1	0	1	0	1	0	1	0	4	0	4
3/2	1	0	1	0	0	1	0	1	2	2	0	0
3/3	1	0	1	0	0	1	0	1	2	2	0	0
3/6	1	0	1	0	0	1	0	1	2	2	0	0
3/7	1	0	1	0	1	0	0	1	3	1	2	0
3/8	1	0	1	0	1	0	0	1	3	1	2	0
3/9	1	0	1	0	1	0	0	1	3	1	2	0
3/10	1	0	1	0	1	0	1	0	4	0	4	0
3/13	1	0	1	0	1	0	1	0	4	0	4	0
3/14	1	0	1	0	1	0	1	0	4	0	4	0
3/15	1	0	1	0	1	0	1	0	4	0	4	0
3/16	0	1	1	0	1	0	1	0	3	1	2	0
3/17	0	1	1	0	1	0	1	0	3	1	2	0
3/20	1	0	1	0	1	0	1	0	4	0	4	0
3/21	1	0	1	0	1	0	1	0	4	0	4	0
3/22	1	0	1	0	1	0	1	0	4	0	4	0
3/23	1	0	1	0	1	0	1	0	4	0	4	0
3/24	1	0	1	0	1	0	1	0	4	0	4	0
3/27	1	0	1	0	1	0	1	0	4	0	4	0
3/28	1	0	1	0	1	0	1	0	4	0	4	0
3/29	1	0	1	0	1	0	1	0	4	0	4	0
3/30	1	0	1	0	1	0	1	0	4	0	4	0
4/3	1	0	1	0	1	0	1	0	4	0	4	0
4/4	1	0	1	0	1	0	1	0	4	0	4	0
4/5	1	0	1	0	1	0	1	0	4	0	4	0
4/6	1	0	1	0	1	0	1	0	4	0	4	0
4/7	1	0	1	0	1	0	1	0	4	0	4	0

Date 1972	CPC-9		CPC-13		CPC-21		25 x 8		TOTAL		NET	
	Long	Short	Long	Short	Long	Short	Long	Short	Long	Short	Long	Short
4/10	1	0	1	0	1	0	1	0	4	0	4	0
4/11	0	1	1	0	1	0	1	0	3	1	2	0
4/12	0	1	1	0	1	0	1	0	3	1	2	0
4/13	0	1	1	0	1	0	1	0	3	1	2	0
4/14	0	1	0	1	1	0	1	0	2	2	0	0
4/17	0	1	0	1	1	0	1	0	2	2	0	0
4/18	0	1	0	1	1	0	1	0	2	2	0	0
4/19	0	1	0	1	0	1	1	0	1	3	0	2
4/20	0	1	0	1	0	1	0	1	0	4	0	4
4/21	0	1	0	1	0	1	0	1	0	4	0	4
4/24	0	1	0	1	0	1	0	1	0	4	0	4
4/25	0	1	0	1	0	1	0	1	0	4	0	4
4/26	0	1	0	1	0	1	0	1	0	4	0	4
4/27	1	0	0	1	0	1	0	1	1	3	0	2
4/28	1	0	0	1	0	1	0	1	1	3	0	2
5/1	1	0	1	0	0	1	0	1	2	2	0	0
5/2	1	0	1	0	0	1	0	1	2	2	0	0
5/3	1	0	1	0	0	1	0	1	2	2	0	0
5/4	1	0	1	0	0	1	0	1	2	2	0	0
5/5	1	0	1	0	0	1	1	0	3	1	2	0
5/8	1	0	1	0	0	1	1	0	3	1	2	0
5/9	1	0	1	0	1	0	1	0	4	0	4	0
5/10	0	1	1	0	1	0	1	0	3	1	2	0
5/11	0	1	1	0	1	0	1	0	3	1	2	0
5/12	0	1	1	0	1	0	1	0	3	1	2	0
5/15	0	1	1	0	1	0	1	0	3	1	2	0
5/16	1	0	1	0	1	0	1	0	4	0	4	0
5/17	1	0	1	0	1	0	1	0	4	0	4	0
5/18	0	1	0	1	1	0	1	0	2	2	0	0
5/19	0	1	0	1	1	0	1	0	2	2	0	0
5/22	0	1	0	1	1	0	1	0	2	2	0	0
5/23	0	1	0	1	0	1	1	0	1	3	0	2
5/24	0	1	0	1	0	1	1	0	1	3	0	2
5/25	0	1	0	1	0	1	0	1	0	4	0	4
5/26	0	1	0	1	0	1	0	1	0	4	0	4
5/30	0	1	0	1	0	1	0	1	0	4	0	4

188

Date 1972	CPC-9		CPC-13		CPC-21		25 x 8		TOTAL		NET	
	Long	Short	Long	Short	Long	Short	Long	Short	Long	Short	Long	Short
5/31	0	1	0	1	0	1	0	1	0	4	0	4
6/1	0	1	0	1	0	1	0	1	0	4	0	4
6/2	0	1	0	1	0	1	0	1	0	4	0	4
6/5	0	1	0	1	0	1	0	1	0	4	0	4
6/6	1	0	0	1	0	1	0	1	1	3	0	2
6/7	1	0	0	1	0	1	0	1	1	3	0	2
6/8	1	0	0	1	0	1	0	1	1	3	0	2
6/9	1	0	0	1	0	1	0	1	1	3	0	2
6/12	1	0	1	0	0	1	0	1	2	2	0	0
6/13	1	0	1	0	0	1	0	1	2	2	0	0
6/14	1	0	1	0	0	1	0	1	2	2	0	0
6/15	1	0	1	0	0	1	1	0	3	1	2	0
6/16	1	0	1	0	0	1	1	0	3	1	2	0
6/19	0	1	1	0	0	1	1	0	2	2	0	0
6/20	0	1	0	1	0	1	1	0	1	3	0	2
6/21	0	1	0	1	0	1	1	0	1	3	0	2
6/22	0	1	0	1	0	1	1	0	1	3	0	2
6/23	0	1	0	1	0	1	1	0	1	3	0	2
6/26	0	1	0	1	0	1	0	1	0	4	0	4
6/27	0	1	0	1	0	1	0	1	0	4	0	4
6/28	0	1	0	1	0	1	0	1	0	4	0	4
6/29	0	1	0	1	0	1	0	1	0	4	0	4
6/30	1	0	0	1	0	1	0	1	1	3	0	2
7/5	1	0	1	0	1	0	0	1	3	1	2	0
7/6	1	0	1	0	1	0	1	0	4	0	4	0
7/7	1	0	1	0	1	0	1	0	4	0	4	0
7/10	1	0	1	0	1	0	1	0	4	0	4	0
7/11	1	0	1	0	1	0	1	0	4	0	4	0
7/12	1	0	1	0	1	0	1	0	4	0	4	0
7/13	1	0	1	0	1	0	1	0	4	0	4	0
7/14	1	0	1	0	1	0	1	0	4	0	4	0
7/17	1	0	1	0	1	0	1	0	4	0	4	0
7/18	1	0	1	0	1	0	1	0	4	0	4	0
7/19	1	0	1	0	1	0	1	0	4	0	4	0
7/20	1	0	1	0	1	0	1	0	4	0	4	0
7/21	1	0	1	0	1	0	1	0	4	0	4	0

Date 1972	CPC-9		CPC-13		CPC-21		25 x 8		TOTAL		NET	
	Long	Short	Long	Short	Long	Short	Long	Short	Long	Short	Long	Short
7/24	1	0	1	0	1	0	1	0	4	0	4	0
7/25	1	0	1	0	1	0	1	0	4	0	4	0
7/26	1	0	1	0	1	0	1	0	4	0	4	0
7/27	0	1	1	0	1	0	1	0	3	1	2	0
7/28	1	0	1	0	1	0	1	0	4	0	4	0
7/31	1	0	1	0	1	0	1	0	4	0	4	0
8/1	1	0	1	0	1	0	1	0	4	0	4	0
8/2	1	0	1	0	1	0	1	0	4	0	4	0
8/3	1	0	1	0	1	0	1	0	4	0	4	0
8/4	1	0	1	0	1	0	1	0	4	0	4	0
8/7	1	0	1	0	1	0	1	0	4	0	4	0
8/8	1	0	1	0	1	0	1	0	4	0	4	0
8/9	0	1	1	0	1	0	1	0	3	1	2	0
8/10	0	1	1	0	1	0	1	0	3	1	2	0
8/11	0	1	1	0	1	0	1	0	3	1	2	0
8/14	0	1	1	0	1	0	1	0	3	1	2	0
8/15	0	1	1	0	1	0	1	0	3	1	2	0
8/16	1	0	1	0	1	0	1	0	4	0	4	0
8/17	1	0	1	0	1	0	1	0	4	0	4	0
8/18	1	0	1	0	1	0	1	0	4	0	4	0
8/21	1	0	1	0	1	0	1	0	4	0	4	0
8/22	1	0	1	0	1	0	1	0	4	0	4	0
8/23	1	0	1	0	1	0	1	0	4	0	4	0
8/24	1	0	1	0	1	0	1	0	4	0	4	0
8/25	1	0	1	0	1	0	1	0	4	0	4	0
8/28	1	0	1	0	1	0	1	0	4	0	4	0
8/29	1	0	1	0	1	0	1	0	4	0	4	0